Greek Mythology

Captivating Greek Myths of Greek Gods, Goddesses, Monsters and Heroes

Free Bonus from Captivating History (Available for a Limited time)

Hi History Lovers!

Now you have a chance to join our exclusive history list so you can get your first history ebook for free as well as discounts and a potential to get more history books for free! Simply visit the link below to join.

Captivatinghistory.com/ebook

Also, make sure to follow us on:
Twitter: @Captivhistory
Facebook: Captivating History:@captivatinghistory

Contents

Introduction

Giants. Gods. Heroes. Monsters. These are the stuff of Greek myths and legends. These ancient stories tell the tales of the before-time, when the heavens and the earth were new, and when great deeds were done by beings who were larger than life.

The ancient Greeks had no concept of a unitary creator-god or set of creator-gods. For the ancient Greeks, the world simply came into being out of Nothingness. But for the Greeks, that Nothingness was in itself a being: the name of the first primordial god, Chaos, in fact, means "Chasm" or "Abyss," and into this abyss Mother Earth also came into being, unmade and unassisted. Greek creation myths also differ from those of for example the book of Genesis in that it's not only plants and animals that come into being through the actions of the gods. Things like Night, Death, Sleep, and Memory also were considered sentient beings that had their places in the ladder of creation and that deserved respect—if not worship—of mortal humans.

In addition to explaining how creation itself began, myths in many cultures have the function of "just-so" stories, explaining various other important things—the invention of fire, why we have weather, the names of plants and birds. Greek mythology is no different: enfolded in grand stories of gods and heroes are some of the ways the ancient Greeks understood many of the more common aspects of their world.

The world was a dangerous place for the ancient Greeks. Disease and famine, war and death were always around the corner and waiting to strike when one least expected it. The ancient Greeks thought that misfortune was the result of the caprice of the gods. Therefore, these myths also function as cautionary tales, warning humans of the sin of hubris, telling them to be humble and worship the gods as was just and right, so that maybe the gods would smile and take pity on the mortals they ruled.

Although the gods and goddesses were powerful immortal beings, they were in many ways still very like the humans who worshiped them and who created these tales. The gods and goddesses are stricken with jealousy; they fall in love; they get angry when they feel slighted, and bestow gifts when they are honored. Likewise, the heroes are larger than life: they're stronger, faster, and more skilled than ordinary mortals, but they are still subject to pain, illness, and death.

There are usually several different versions of these myths, which were told and retold over a span of many centuries. The versions presented here are an amalgamation from various ancient Greek sources. My goal has not been to create an "official" text, so sometimes I have mingled variants from different sources to create a single compelling narrative that at the same time is faithful to ancient ways of remembering these stories, which still have so much to tell us even today.

Part I

The Golden Age of the Titans

The Creation of the Titans

In the beginning, there was only Chaos. Out of Chaos came Darkness and Night. Night was mother to both Air and Day, but also to Doom, Death, Sleep, and Old Age, and many other children besides, and Darkness was their father.

After Chaos came Gaia, who is Mother Earth, and then Eros, the god of love. Gaia herself brought forth Uranus, that is Father Sky, and with him, Gaia made the first and oldest gods, the Titans, who governed the universe and peopled it with their divine children. Some of these children were fair beings, who themselves gave birth to gods and goddesses, but others were fearsome to behold. These were the Cyclops, great giants with only one eye each, and the Hecatoncheires, the Hundred-Handed Ones, three brothers with fifty heads and one hundred arms each. Father Sky feared the Cyclops and the Hecatoncheires. He captured them and imprisoned them in Tartarus, a terrible, dark cavern deep under the earth, from which nothing could escape.

Besides the Cyclops and Hundred-Handed Ones, together Mother Earth and Father Sky had twelve children, six males, who were Oceanus, Hyperion, Coeus, Cronus, Crius, and Iapetus; and six females, Mnemosyne (Memory), Tethys, Theia, Phoebe, Rhea, and Themis.

Uranus was jealous of his children and hid them away in a cavern deep inside Gaia. As Uranus put each child inside their mother, Gaia began to feel the pain of over-fullness, so she went and created a great sickle of adamant, the hardest of all metals, and showed it to her children.

"Which of you will take this sickle, and free us from Father Sky's oppression?" said Mother Earth.

But Gaia's children were all terrified of their father, and none would step forward to take the sickle, until one day Cronus said, "Give me the sickle, Mother. I will do as you ask."

Gaia hid Cronus away where Uranus would not see him and told him what he should do. As the day ended, Father Sky came to Mother Earth, covering her with night and wanting to make love to her. And when Uranus was stretched out over the fair Earth, Cronus took the sickle of adamant and cut his father's genitals off. Cronus cast these away behind him. Drops of Uranus' blood landed on Gaia and were taken into her, and from these were made the Furies, Alecto, Tisiphone, and Magaera, the goddesses of vengeance; and the Giants; and the nymphs of the trees.

Uranus' genitals landed in the ocean. As they floated on the water, white foam began to grow around them. The white foam grew and took the shape of a young woman, the purest and most beautiful of all. She stepped out of the water onto the island of Cyprus and is called Aphrodite, the goddess of love. Aphrodite had two helpers at her birth: Eros, the god of love, and Himeros, god of desire, who was born with her.

Once the Titans were all freed from the cavern, they took one another as husbands and wives and began to make children of their own. The Sun, Moon, and the Dawn were all children of Hyperion and Theia. Oceanus, the great sea that encircles the whole world, and his wife Tethys, were the parents of many mighty rivers, including the Nile and the Danube, and of Metis, the first wife of Zeus and mother of Athena, goddess of wisdom. Atlas, who holds the sky on his shoulders, and Prometheus, bringer of fire, and ill-fated Epimetheus were the sons of Iapetus and Asia, who herself was an Oceanid, a daughter of Oceanus and Tethys. Many of these Titans and children of Titans have stories of their own, some of which will be told later.

The Birth of the Olympians and the Downfall of the Titans

By far the most important descendants of the Titans were the Olympians, children of Rhea and Cronus, who eventually overthrew the older gods and came to rule over all creation from the heights of Mount Olympus, with Father Zeus at their head. And this is how that came to pass.

Rhea and Cronus, Titans both and children of Mother Earth and Father Sky, lived as husband and wife, and Rhea bore Cronus many children. But Cronus was jealous and grasping and had heard his reign over all that was would be ended by one of his children. Every time Rhea bore him a child, Cronus snatched it away and ate it, first Hestia, then Demeter, Hera, Hades, and Poseidon, one after the other, thinking that would protect him and secure his throne forever.

This made Rhea deeply sorrowful, so the next time she felt herself with child, she begged her parents, Mother Earth and Father Sky, for help. They agreed to help her, guiding her to a cave on the island of Crete, where Zeus was born and where Rhea hid her son far, far away within Gaia. There Zeus lived, cared for by his grandmother until he was grown.

After Rhea left Zeus in the cave, she swaddled a rock to make it look like a baby, and brought it to Cronus, saying, "See, here is your new-born son."

Cronus was so hasty in his jealousy and fear he swallowed the rock whole, without even looking at it. Then he was satisfied, thinking that he could never be overthrown since he had imprisoned every one of his children inside himself.

Meanwhile, in the cave on the island of Crete, Zeus grew in stature and might, and when he deemed the time was right, he left the cave and went searching for his father. He found mighty Cronus, and they had a fierce battle. Zeus was too strong for wicked Cronus and forced him to vomit up all his brothers and sisters. The first thing Cronus vomited up was the rock he had swallowed in Zeus' place. Then out came Poseidon, Hades, Hera, Demeter, and Hestia, one after the other. The rock Zeus kept, as a memorial to his victory, and had it placed in Pytho, on holy Mount Parnassus.

It became clear to Zeus that something needed to be done about who wielded power in the universe. Was it to be the old gods, the Titans? Or was it to be the younger gods and goddesses, the Olympians, who were his brothers and sisters? Clearly the Titans were not to be trusted: Zeus' father had eaten his children, after all, and Zeus had escaped that fate himself only through the courage and resourcefulness of his mother. Zeus knew he was strong, and so were his brothers and sisters, but he also knew he would need help. The first ones he decided to call upon were the Cyclops, terrible, one-eyed giants named Brontes (Thunderer), Steropes (Lightning), and Arges (Brightness), all of whom were gifted makers and smiths.

Now, the Cyclops had been imprisoned in Tartarus, a terrible, dark cavern far below the earth, from which there was no escape. Uranus, Father Sky, had placed them there for the first time, long ago, and there they stayed, until Cronus, father of the Olympian gods, freed them and asked them to help him overthrow Uranus. The Cyclops helped Cronus with a good will, and Uranus was overthrown, but wicked Cronus double-crossed the Cyclops: as soon as they were no longer of any use to him, he imprisoned them in Tartarus once again.

Zeus braved the terrible deeps of Tartarus and freed the Cyclops from their prison. In thanks for their freedom, they made thunder and lightning and gave these to Zeus, which he could then use in his battles with the Titans or whenever else he might have need of them. The Cyclops also bestowed a trident upon Poseidon and gave a helmet to Hades.

The Cyclops were not the only ones who Zeus freed from Tartarus. The Hecatoncheires, the Hundred-Handed Ones, Cottus (Furious), Briareus (Vigorous), and Gyges (Big-Limbed) were three sons of Uranus, and their mother was Gaia. These brothers each had fifty heads and a hundred arms and were fearsomely strong and brave in battle. These three brothers also had been imprisoned in Tartarus by Father Sky, and it was Rhea, mother of Zeus, who gave her son the idea to free these three brothers also, saying that if Zeus released them, he could call upon them for help when he needed it. Zeus followed his mother's advice. He descended again into the pit of Tartarus and freed the Hundred-Handed Ones who, as Rhea had said, then promised to fight for Zeus whenever he called.

With the weapons of the Cyclops and the help of the Hundred-Handed Ones, Zeus and the Olympians went to war against the Titans. There was a mighty battle, and in the end, the Titans were defeated. Zeus then imprisoned them in Tartarus and set the Hundred-Handed Ones to guard them. The next thing to be done was to divide up the rule of the universe. Zeus, the god of thunder and lightning, took the sky. Poseidon, the god of the sea, took the oceans and seas, and Hades was allotted the Underworld, the place of the Dead which also bears his name.

Prometheus and Epimetheus

Prometheus was the son of the Titan Iapetus and Clymene, daughter of Oceanus and Tethys, and Epimetheus was his brother. Prometheus fought on the side of the Olympians during their struggle against the Titans, and so never was imprisoned in Tartarus. Some say that Prometheus was the creator of mankind, fashioning human beings out of mud alongside his brother, Epimetheus and that they also made the animals, birds, and fish.

The brothers worked together to shape all the beasts and birds and fish. Epimetheus gave to them various gifts: feathers or fur; flight or crawling upon the earth; strength, swiftness, wisdom. When the creatures were all shaped and given their gifts, Athena breathed life into them. But when it came time for Prometheus to make humans, he found that Epimetheus had already given all the good things to the other animals, and the only things left to give the humans were the ability to walk upright, just as the gods and goddesses themselves did, and the gift of fire.

Prometheus loved the humans more than anything else, and although he had fought with the Olympians against the Titans, he was still angry with Zeus for imprisoning his family in the horrible pit of Tartarus. One day, as Prometheus thought to teach the humans how to make sacrifice to great Zeus, and to teach that mighty god a lesson. The humans sacrificed a bull to Zeus, and Prometheus told them to make two piles, one with the bones covered by a mound of fat, and the other with the choice parts of the meat wrapped up in the animal's hide. Prometheus told Zeus, "You can have first choice, but that will be what you accept from the humans for the rest of time."

Zeus suspected a trick, but he agreed to Prometheus' conditions. He looked at the two portions, one that was a lump covered in hide, the other a mound of luscious fat. Zeus took the portion with the fat but was enraged when he found that underneath it was no meat, but just a pile of bones. Even though he was very angry, Zeus kept his word, and from then on when humans made sacrifice to him, they gave him the fat and the bones, and he accepted that from them.

However, Zeus felt he could not let that trick go unpunished: he took fire away from the humans. The poor humans shivered in their homes, unable to warm themselves and growing thin because they could not cook their food. Prometheus took pity on them and decided to give fire back to them, no matter what Zeus might think or do. Prometheus took a great torch and lit it by holding it against the sun. He then brought the fire back to the humans, who rejoiced that they could once again warm their homes and cook their food and do all the other many things they needed fire to do.

Zeus saw this and decided to punish both Prometheus and humankind. But that wasn't the only reason he was angry with Prometheus: Prometheus had also said that one of Zeus' children would overthrow him and refused to say who it would be. In order to punish Prometheus, first Zeus ordered two of his servants, Violence, and Authority, to go with the smith-god Hephaestus to take Prometheus and chain him to a great rock in the Caucasus Mountains with a diamond chain that not even the son of a Titan could break. Then Zeus sent a giant eagle to eat Prometheus' liver every day. Since Prometheus was an immortal god, his liver grew back every time afterward, and so he suffered and could not die.

Zeus said that he would let Prometheus go if either he told Zeus who would dethrone him, or if a mortal offered to die in his place. Some say that Prometheus eventually was set free when the centaur Chiron agreed to die for Prometheus and the mighty hero Heracles helped set him free by capturing the eagle and killing it, and by breaking the chains. But Prometheus never told Zeus who it was that would overthrow him: that secret he kept forever.

The great god Zeus never got over his shame at Prometheus' trick with the bones and the fat, nor of his jealousy over humans getting fire back. Once Zeus had bound Prometheus to his rock and set upon him the eagle, he next turned his attention to Prometheus' brother, Epimetheus, who had helped in the creation of the humans who had helped Prometheus work mighty Zeus' humiliation at the sacrifice. If Prometheus and his humans could play a trick on Zeus, then Zeus could do the same to Epimetheus, and Zeus went about it this way: first, he went to Hephaestus and told him to make a human woman more beautiful than any other on earth. Then Zeus took the woman to Hermes, and told him to make her untrustworthy, and to make her a liar. They called this woman Pandora. Zeus also gave Pandora a box that she was told she must never, ever open.

Zeus took Pandora down to the Earth, where Epimetheus had been living among the humans. Zeus gave Pandora to Epimetheus as a gift. Epimetheus remembered that his brother had told him not to trust Zeus, and never to accept any gifts from him, but Pandora was so beautiful Epimetheus couldn't help himself: he accepted her gladly and took her to be his wife.

For a time, Pandora and Epimetheus lived happily together, but the mysterious box preyed on Pandora's mind. She wondered repeatedly what was inside it. What if she took just a little peek? What if she opened the box only the very tiniest crack? Surely nothing bad would come of that.

Pandora thought about it and thought about it. She couldn't banish thoughts of the box from her head. So, one day, when Epimetheus had gone out, she took the box down from its shelf. She set it on a table and very slowly, very carefully, she opened it the tiniest of cracks. But her care in opening it didn't matter: the box was filled with all the evils of the world—Fear, Disease, Hunger, Pain, Envy, Spite, and all manner of other foul things—and they were so numerous and so strong that they pushed the lid wide open and escaped out into the world to plague mankind. Pandora closed the box as quickly as she could, but not before all the things had escaped except one: Hope. And that is why humans still have hope, even in a world that is full of death and sickness and woe.

The Birth of the Muses

One time Zeus saw Mnemosyne, Titan daughter of Mother Earth and Father Sky, and he desired her greatly. So, Zeus came to her once a night for nine nights, and soon she found herself pregnant. When her time came, Mnemosyne gave birth to nine beautiful daughters. These daughters grew up to be beautiful women, skilled in many arts, and they are the ones that humans call on for help when they wish for inspiration, and they are known together as the Muses.

Calliope was the eldest, and it is she who encourages men to write tales of gods and heroes and to sing of great deeds. Clio is the Muse of history, of the telling of true stories of kings and empires, while Euterpe helps men write music and lyric poetry. When a man is in love and wants to write a poem for his beloved, he calls upon Erato, whose skill is in the verse of love, while dramatists call on Melponeme for tragedy and Thalia for comedy. Polyhmnia gives humans the ability to write good songs in praise of the almighty gods, while Terpsichore teaches them to dance with grace and joy. And finally, Urania is the Muse of astronomy, helping humans to learn and understand the motions of the heavens and what these mean to people on Earth.

It may seem odd to us today to consider the study of astronomy among all these other literary and musical arts, but it wouldn't have been seen this way by people in ancient Greece. Whereas we think of things like "melody" as the tune of a musical piece, and of "harmony" as musical chords or adding a second voice part to a melody, the ancient Greeks had a much broader and more complex understanding of those terms that went far beyond things like songs or instrumental music. The ancient Greek concept of "melos" (which is where we get our word "melody") encompassed the text, the rhythm, and sometimes even the dance movements that went along with a particular piece. And "harmony" wasn't just a pleasing way of making chords or having different musical lines work with each other: it also encompassed the idea of proper relationships among human beings, and between human beings and the universe at large.

This concept of connections between music and the structure of society and the universe was so powerful that it led many philosophers to suppose that the structure of the universe was itself musical. The idea that each planet creates its own kind of musical hum, and that these hums can be expressed as musical intervals from one planet to the other, is often attributed to the Greek mathematician Pythagoras and was an accepted way of understanding the universe well into the Renaissance.

For one of the Muses to be associated with the study of the heavens and the structure of the universe, while her sisters all deal in music and poetry of different kinds, is therefore not surprising. The harmony of the universe and the place of humans within it was just as much a musical thing to ancient people as the songs they sang or tunes they danced to.

Part II

The Olympian Gods and Goddesses

We have heard much of the deeds of Father Zeus, how he defeated the Titans and chained Prometheus, and did many other mighty things. Now we turn our thoughts to the other Olympian gods, the siblings and children of great Zeus.

Hera, Queen of the Gods

Hera was the daughter of Rhea and Cronus, the third wife of mighty Father Zeus, goddess of women, of marriage, and of the sky. Hera bore Zeus three children, of whom the most famous was violent Ares, god of war. She was the foster-daughter of Tethys, who cared for her at the time that Zeus and his brothers were fighting the Titans. Some say that when the battle with the Titans was done, Hera, Poseidon, and Hades became afraid of Zeus in his great power and tried to chain him. He was set free when Thetys went to Briareus, one of the Hundred-Handed Ones, who came to Olympus and stood by Zeus' side. After that, the other gods didn't dare try to chain Zeus again.

Zeus had already had several wives and fathered many children by the time he married Hera, and his wandering ways did not stop once they were wed. Hera suffered much from the infidelities of Zeus. Her jealousy led her to create a son of her own, crafty Hephaestus, and she often tried to destroy Zeus' other children, even that greatest of heroes and her namesake, the mighty Heracles himself.

Hera was not without her admirers, although she did not welcome them. The story is told of a man named Ixion, who desired Hera and pressed his attention on her. Hera did not want this, and so told Zeus. Zeus then tricked Ixion by presenting him with a cloud made into Hera's likeness. Ixion thought this was Hera and so made love to it. Some say that from Ixion's union with the cloud was born the first centaur. But even though Ixion had not slept with Hera herself, his presumption could not go unpunished. Zeus therefore fixed him to a wheel and doomed him to go spinning through the air, pushed by the winds, for all eternity.

Hermes, Trickster, and Messenger of the Gods

Atlas was the son of Iapetus and brother of Prometheus, and his wife was Pleione, daughter of Ocean. Together they had seven daughters, the Pleiades, one of whom was named Maia. Zeus looked upon Maia and desired her, and so he made love to her. Soon she became pregnant and gave birth to a baby boy, whom she named Hermes.

Now, Hermes was a precocious lad, and even when he was an infant, he started playing tricks. The first trick he played was on the god Apollo. Hermes left the cave where he had been living with his mother and went to Pieria where he stole a herd of cattle belonging to the elder god. To cover his tracks, he put shoes on the feet of the cattle to confuse their tracks. Hermes took the cattle to Pylus, where he sacrificed some of them, then ate some of the flesh and burned the rest. The cattle he did not sacrifice he hid inside a cave.

When he had finished this deed, he sat for a while outside the cave. After a time, he noticed a tortoise making its slow way across the grass. Hermes caught the tortoise and killed it. He scraped out the inside of its shell and put strings across it. In this way, Hermes invented the lyre. He also designed a plectrum to use to play it.

Meanwhile, Apollo learned of Hermes' theft of his cattle, and he went looking for the young god so he could get them back. He went to Hermes' mother and accused her son of stealing the cattle. But Maia held up the infant Hermes and said, "How could this small baby have stolen a herd of cattle?"

But Apollo wasn't fooled. He took Hermes before Zeus and told him about the theft of the cattle. At first, Hermes denied he had the animals, but eventually, he relented and took Apollo to the cave where he had hidden them. The lyre Hermes had made was at the cave, too. Apollo asked what it was, so Hermes showed him how to play it. Apollo was entranced by this new instrument, so he gave the cattle to Hermes in exchange for it, and that is how Apollo came to be a player of the lyre.

Hermes took the cattle to pasture and cared for them; now they were his own. But watching over the cattle sometimes was boring, so Hermes fashioned a flute for himself to play and thus wile away the time. Apollo heard the flute and went to see what it was. There he found Hermes playing the shepherd's pipe. Apollo asked to have the pipe, but Hermes wouldn't give it to him for the asking: in exchange, he demanded Apollo's golden wand so he would then have the power of divination. Apollo thought it a fair exchange, so he got the flute and Hermes took the golden wand.

Zeus made Hermes his special messenger. Hermes also is the patron of trade, of cattle, and of tricksters.

Grey-Eyed Athena, Goddess of Wisdom and Strategy

Zeus' first wife was Metis, daughter of the Titans Oceanus and Tethys. Metis soon found herself pregnant by Zeus. Mother Earth and Father Sky warned Zeus she would bring forth a child so wise and mighty that he could overthrow his father. This made Zeus very worried. He asked Mother Earth and Father Sky for advice, and they told him he should swallow the child, as his father, Cronus, had done. Zeus decided he wouldn't wait until the child was born. He snatched up pregnant Metis and swallowed her whole.

Metis went up into Zeus' head and gave birth to a fine daughter. Metis then set about weaving a robe and making a helmet for her child. The incessant hammering on the helmet gave Zeus a mighty headache. Nothing he did could make it stop. In agony, he begged the other gods for help. Finally, great Prometheus took an ax and swung it right down the middle of Zeus' head, although some say that this was Hephaestus' doing. From the wound sprang a goddess, fully grown, dressed in a beautiful robe and armed with a helmet. This was Zeus' daughter, Athena, goddess of wisdom, justice, and strategy, and the city of Athens is named for her and under her particular protection, and this is how that came to be.

Once there was a king named Cecrops, and he founded a great city. Some say that Cecrops was not a human man, but rather had the upper body of a man and the tail of a great serpent or fish instead of legs. Some also say that Cecrops was the first one to offer sacrifice to Zeus and to declare him a god after the defeat of the Titans. Cecrops wanted a patron god or goddess for his city, so he offered to let the Olympians vie for that honor. Poseidon and Athena decided that they would enter the contest. Poseidon walked to the top of the Acropolis, the great stone hill in the center of the city and struck the ground with his great trident. A gush of pure, clear water came bubbling out, symbolizing that Poseidon could give Athens enormous power over the seas, and a mighty navy. Athena planted an olive tree, symbolizing peace and prosperity. Cecrops consulted with the people of the city as to which deity they wished as the patron of their city, and the people said, "We want Athena." And so, the city was named Athens, and the people took the goddess Athena to be their protectress, building her a fine temple atop the Acropolis.

Athena bestowed her favor on those who honored her, and destruction and disgrace on those who did not, but she always judged fairly. One story tells of a young man named Tiresias, whose mother was a nymph. One day, Tiresias came upon the goddess Athena where she was bathing. Tiresias hadn't meant to intrude, but the virgin goddess was angry that a man had seen her naked, and so struck Tiresias blind. Tiresias' mother vouched for her son and begged the goddess to restore his sight, but she could not do so. Instead, Athena cleaned his ears with a woolen cloth, after which Tiresias could understand the speech of birds. With this understanding, Tiresias became a famous and mighty seer and prophet.

This goddess, wise in strategy, also favored those who work with skill and craft. Once there was a boy named Perdix who was an apprentice to the builder Daedalus. Perdix was a great observer of nature and tried to make useful things based on what he had seen. One day he looked at the backbone of a fish. Then he went and got a sheet of iron and cut teeth into one edge, in imitation of the ridges in the fish's spine. He discovered this edge could cut wood very easily: Perdix had invented the saw. But his master, Daedalus, was very jealous of his apprentice's talent. He seized Perdix and threw him over the edge of the Acropolis, but made it look like Perdix had fallen by accident. Athena saw the boy as he was falling, and rescued Perdix by turning him into a bird. Perdix even kept his own name afterward, since "Perdix" means "partridge."

Hephaestus, God of Fire and Smithcraft

When Hera saw Zeus had given birth to wise, grey-eyed Athena, she was jealous and vowed to get her own back by producing a child without the aid of either Zeus or any other. Soon Hera gave birth to a baby boy, whom she named Hephaestus. But Hera was disgusted by the child because its legs were shriveled. She therefore threw the young Hephaestus down from Olympus. But Eurynome, daughter of Oceanus, and Thetys, daughter of Nereus, caught the baby. They took him into their home, and there he began to show his great skill at working with metal, making all manner of weapons and armor and jewelry.

Hephaestus was angry that Hera had barred him from Olympus and vowed to find a way to rejoin the other gods. He therefore made a special chair that he sent up to Hera as a gift, but in fact the chair was cursed: anyone but Hera might sit in it and come to no harm, but if the Queen of Olympus sat in it, there she would be bound fast until Hephaestus saw fit to let her go.

The chair was brought up to Olympus, and soon enough Hera decided to sit in it. There she was caught fast. Some say that Zeus offered the hand of Aphrodite to the one who would release her, and this tale is told in the story of Ares, the God of War. Others say the other gods and goddesses went to Hephaestus and urged him to come to Olympus to set her free since she was his mother, and that Hephaestus refused until Dionysus got him drunk and brought him back to the abode of the gods. There Hephaestus released Hera from the cursed chair, and he was welcomed back into Olympus.

Hephaestus continued his metalworking even after his return to the abode of the gods, and he would make things for those who asked. Some things he made were good, such as the armor worn by Achilles when he went to fight on the shores of Troy; others he made caused suffering, such as the chains of Prometheus and the young woman Pandora, who released so many woes upon the world.

Artemis, Virgin Goddess of the Hunt

Leto was the daughter of the Titans Coeus and Phoebe. Zeus desired her and took her to be his wife. Soon Leto became pregnant with twins, a boy, and a girl. The boy she named Apollo and the girl she named Artemis.

Artemis loved wild animals, and she loved the hunt. Although many desired her, she had no wish to take a lover or to be married, so she went to Father Zeus and asked that she be permitted to remain a virgin forever. Artemis also asked of mighty Zeus a bow and arrows, a tunic that came to the knee so she could run and hunt, and the company of many nymphs who would be her friends and helpers, and who would care for her hunting dogs. Zeus loved Artemis greatly, and so granted her these wishes. Her bow and arrows were made by none other than the Cyclops, the great makers, and smiths who forge thunderbolts for mighty Zeus. The hounds of Artemis were no ordinary dogs: they were a gift of the god Pan, who gave her seven good dogs of his very own, swift to the hunt, and unafraid even of lions. Artemis also desired a chariot to take her to and fro, so she chased after five golden-antlered deer that were strong and tireless and as large as bulls. She was only able to capture four of them; the fifth escaped and ran into the Ceryneian hills and was only captured again when great Heracles did his mighty deeds.

Thus, Artemis became the protectress of wild animals and hunters, of young maidens and children. She also was sacred to women in childbirth, because it is said that when the time came for Leto to have her babies, Artemis was born first, and then helped her mother with the delivery of her brother.

Artemis jealously guarded her virginity, and let no male come near her, whether man or god. One day the hunter Actaeon came upon Artemis and her nymphs when they were bathing, and instead of turning away Actaeon decided to spy upon them. When Artemis caught him, she turned him into a deer and set his own dogs on him. The dogs hunted Actaeon, leaped upon him, and killed him, a punishment for his forwardness in gazing upon Artemis while she was naked.

Although Artemis never took either lover or husband, she did have male friends. One of these was Orion, a great hunter, and giant. Orion boasted he could kill any animal that walked upon the earth, no matter how fearsome. Mother Earth heard this and was angered. She sent a great scorpion to attack Orion. The scorpion stung him on the heel, and Orion died from the poison. Artemis grieved her friend's death and appealed to the Olympian gods to place him in the heavens. The gods heard her plea and put both Orion and the fatal scorpion in the sky as constellations.

Apollo, God of Music and Healing

Apollo was the son of Leto and mighty Zeus, and the twin brother of Artemis, goddess of the hunt. Like his sister, Apollo demanded a bow and arrows, but he also took up the lyre Hermes had made, so that he might make music and create songs. Apollo became the most accomplished musician among all the Olympians and the patron god of those who sing and play music. Apollo is the enforcer of Zeus' will, and it is his arrows that bring death and sickness to men when they disobey or anger the eternal gods, but he has equal power to heal and refresh, and sometimes will take away illness from those who beg his mercy and worship him with proper sacrifice.

The Oracle of Delphi was sacred to golden Apollo, and this is how it came to be his. Long, long ago, in the beginning of the world, Gaia, that is Mother Earth, came to Delphi. She saw that the place was sacred because this was where almighty Zeus had set the stone that Rhea tricked Cronos into swallowing in place of the infant Zeus. So, Mother Earth set a great serpent named Python to guard the stone from all who would trespass there.

Some say that Apollo was angry at Python because the serpent had chased his mother when she was pregnant with him; others say that he wanted access to the oracle, but Python would not let him pass. Either way, Apollo decided that Python was his enemy and needed to be destroyed, so he took his bow and shot her through with arrows. When the serpent was dead, Apollo took possession of the oracle, and from then on it was a place sacred to him.

Like Zeus, his father, Apollo sometimes fell in love with mortals. He was especially enamored of a young man named Hyacinth. Hyacinth was the most beautiful of all men, with a well-made body and thick, dark hair. One day, Apollo was practicing with the discus. His throw went wild, and struck Hyacinth in the head, killing him. Apollo was beside himself with grief for having slain the young man he loved so much. As a memorial to Hyacinth and his beauty, Apollo caused flowers to spring up in the places where Hyacinth's blood had flowed, and the flowers are still named after Apollo's beloved today.

Apollo could love very deeply, but he was also capable of great anger and cruelty. Apollo was jealous of his status as the greatest musician of all, as that satyr, Marsyas found out to his great misery, and this is how that came about. One day the goddess Athena desired to make some music, so she created a new instrument. It had two pipes with reeds in them, and it was played by blowing on the reeds and fingering the holes in the pipes. Athena was very pleased with her new instrument, which she called an *aulos,* and went about Olympus making music on it. But the other gods and goddesses laughed at her because of the way she puffed out her cheeks when she was playing it. This made Athena feel ashamed, so she threw the aulos away.

The satyr Marsyas chanced upon the aulos where Athena had thrown it. He picked it up and blew into it. He liked the sound it made, so he taught himself to play songs on it. Soon he was an accomplished musician, able to play many different melodies, and to play them very well. "Ha!" said Marsyas. "I am as good a musician as the great god Apollo himself!"

Apollo heard Marsyas' boast, and it made him angry. Apollo went to him and challenged him to a contest of musical skill. They agreed that the winner would be able to do whatever he wanted to the loser.

Apollo picked up his lyre and played, skillfully and well. Marsyas picked up his aulos and played, ably and well. For a long time, it seemed that neither of them would win. Until Apollo turned his lyre upside down and began to play on it. "Can you play your aulos upside down?" he asked Marsyas.

But Marsyas could not. Apollo was judged the winner of the contest, and the penalty he gave poor Marsyas was to be skinned alive.

Dionysus, God of Wine and Ritual Madness

Semele was the daughter of Cadmus and Harmonia. Zeus fell in love with her and took her to his bed, but he did so secretly, and in the dark, for she was human, and he did not want to hurt her by revealing his true self. Semele wanted to see Zeus in his full glory. She asked him to come to her in the same way he went to his divine wife, Hera. Zeus reluctantly agreed and came to her in thunder and lightning. This caused Semele to miscarry the baby she had by Zeus before she died of fright. Semele had only been six months along, and Zeus did not want the child to die as well, so he took the baby, who was named Dionysus, and sewed it into his thigh until it was old enough to be born. Thus, Dionysus is sometimes referred to as the "twice-born" god.

Zeus gave the baby to Hermes to care for, and Hermes brought him to his mother's sister, Ino, who was married to a man named Athamas. Some say that Hermes persuaded Ino and Athamas to bring Dionysus up as a girl, but that jealous Hera made them go insane, so Zeus rescued the child by turning him into a sheep and sending him to live with the nymphs of Nysa. Others say that Dionysus and his dead mother were placed in a chest, and when they washed up on shore, Ino found them. Ino and her people gave Semele a decent burial, and she brought up the child in safety.

Whatever his upbringing, it was Dionysus who discovered the grapevine and the way to make wine. Some say that Hera also threw Dionysus into a state of madness, out of jealousy over Zeus' dalliance with Semele and that this is why he wandered the world for many years. Dionysus went to Egypt and Syria, then to Phrygia and Thrace. Thrace was at war with India at the time, and Dionysus fought for the Thracians.

Next Dionysus went to Thebes, where he drove the women into a mad frenzy. The men of Thebes did not like this and tried to put a stop to it. Dionysus felt dishonored by this and commanded the women to attack the men. They did so, rending the men limb from limb. A similar thing happened at Argos: when the people there failed to do him honor, he made the women go mad, killing the men and their own infants in their delirium.

Dionysus had a mind to sail to Naxos, so he found a ship that would take them there. But the ship was manned by pirates who, not knowing that Dionysus was a god, conspired to sail to Asia instead and sell him as a slave. Dionysus learned what they were planning, so he turned the mast and oars into snakes and made ivy grow, and the sound of flutes play all over the ship. This drove the pirates mad. They all jumped overboard, and Dionysus turned them into dolphins. Dionysus eventually came to Naxos, where he found the young Ariadne sleeping, and he took her to be his wife, as is told in the story of the great hero Theseus.

Once Dionysus was done with his travels, wherever he went he was accompanied by a great throng of satyrs and wild, young girls called Maenads. And some say that before Dionysus went up into Olympus, he first went down to Hades to find his mother. When he found her, he changed her name to Thyone and brought her to Olympus with him.

Ares, God of War, and Aphrodite, Goddess of Love

Ares was the son of Zeus and Hera. A violent and changeable god, he loved battle and killing and sometimes switched his loyalties from one side to the other. This happened during the great war between Greece and Troy, that started upon the abduction of Helen. When the Trojan war began, Ares fought first on the side of the Greeks, but fair Aphrodite later convinced him to lend his might to the Trojans.

Warriors and those who excelled in the use of weapons were beloved of Ares, and he favored them with gifts. As is told in the tales of the great hero Heracles, to Hippolyta, queen of the Amazons, Ares gave a precious belt; to Diomedes, he gave fierce, flesh-eating horses.

Now, Ares loved the goddess Aphrodite, she who was born from the sea-foam, and she loved him, but they had not yet been bound as man and wife when the smith-god Hephaestus sent the cursed throne in which Queen Hera was bound. Some say that when Hera could not be freed by the efforts of any of the other Olympians, Father Zeus offered fair Aphrodite to be wife of whoever could free Hera. Aphrodite agreed, thinking that surely brave, strong Ares would be able to accomplish this. But nothing Ares did could free Hera from the chair. Finally, Hephaestus came to Olympus, and he freed Hera with ease.

As promised, Hephaestus was given Aphrodite to be his wife. Aphrodite was very unhappy with this. She didn't want to be the wife of crippled Hephaestus. So, one day, when Ares knew Hephaestus was out, he came to Aphrodite, and they went to bed together. They thought they were making love in secret, but Helios, the sun-god, saw them and told Hephaestus. Hephaestus was furious. He went to his forge and made a set of chains, woven in a strong net, with which to capture the lovers. The next time Ares and Aphrodite were together, Hephaestus came into the bedroom and threw the net over them. There the two lovers were trapped; they could not get away.

Hephaestus called all the other gods of Olympus to come and see the lovers' shame. They came, and they laughed at Ares and Aphrodite, all except Poseidon, who asked Hephaestus to let them go, saying that Ares would pay whatever price the smith-god asked. Hephaestus laughed. "Ares is not trustworthy, as you can see. I doubt he will pay a single penny."

But Poseidon insisted. He said that if Ares refused to make good his debt, that he would pay in his stead. So, Hephaestus let Ares and Aphrodite go, and they ran away to live in love on the island of Cyprus, the place where fair Aphrodite first arose from the sea.

Ares and Aphrodite had a daughter, Harmonia, who became the wife of King Cadmus of Illyria and mother to Semele, whom Zeus loved and who was the mother of the god Dionysus. When the Illyrians went to war, Ares fought for them, and Harmonia herself entered the fray among the soldiers, as a daughter of Ares should do.

Ares did not go into war unaccompanied. His charioteers Deimos (Terror) and Phobos (Fear) were ever with him, and some say that these also were children Ares had by Aphrodite. The goddess Eris (Strife), daughter of Night, was often said to be Ares' sister. She also goes with him into battle, making the hate and suffering of mankind even worse.

Aphrodite, the beloved of war-god Ares, was the goddess of love, but like all the Olympians she could become angry if she felt disrespected. Some say that anger at disrespect was the cause of the birth of the lovely youth, Adonis, and this is how that came about. King Thais of Assyria had a daughter, Smyrna, who refused to honor Aphrodite. As a punishment, Aphrodite made Smyrna desire her own father. Smyrna played a trick on Thais that allowed her to share his bed with him for twelve nights, but he was unaware that the woman he slept with was his daughter. When Thais learned how Smyrna had tricked him, he was angry and ashamed. He prayed to the gods that his daughter be punished for her crime, and they granted his wish by turning her into a myrrh tree, and indeed, this was fitting, for the name "Smyrna" means "myrrh."

But Smyrna was with child at the time of this punishment, so when the nine months had passed, the tree burst open and out came a beautiful baby boy, who was called Adonis. Aphrodite saw this and took Adonis to Persephone that he might be looked after, thinking she could get Adonis back later, except Persephone loved the boy and would not give him back when Aphrodite asked. The two goddesses brought the matter before Father Zeus for judgment. Zeus said that Adonis would spend part of the year with Persephone, part with Aphrodite, and part with himself. Adonis was later killed when he went hunting and was gored by the tusks of a boar. Some say that this was the work of Ares, who was jealous of Aphrodite's love for the young man; others say it was a punishment from Artemis because Adonis was such a fine hunter.

The Story of Demeter and Persephone

Persephone was the daughter of Demeter, goddess of the harvest, and Zeus was her father. Persephone was very beautiful, and many of the gods desired her. Apollo asked for her hand, as did Hermes, but Demeter refused them all and took Persephone away to a place where the gods could not find her.

Persephone loved growing things, especially flowers. One day, she was out gathering flowers with her maidens. Persephone especially loved the white narcissus for their delicate blooms and thick, sweet scent. She found a place in the meadow with an abundance of narcissus flowers, and she sat among them to gaze at their beauty.

Now, Hades, the Lord of the Underworld, also had wished to court Persephone but had been prevented by her mother. Hades knew of Persephone's love for the narcissus flower, and so had caused them to grow in that meadow, to lure her to that spot. So, while Persephone sat among the narcissus that Hades had planted, Hades jumped into his chariot that was pulled by many fine black horses. He thundered out of the Underworld and into the meadow, where he snatched up Persephone. Heedless of her cries, Hades drove his chariot back into the Land of the Dead, taking Persephone with him, thinking to make her his wife.

When Demeter learned her daughter had been taken, she searched all over the earth for her. So, stricken was she at the loss of Persephone she neglected the earth. The crops ceased to grow, and the trees ceased to bear fruit. A hard, lean time came for the people and the animals, a time of cold and harsh barrenness.

The people cried out to great Zeus for help, because they were starving. Even the other gods and goddesses begged him to intervene because the earth was no longer hospitable even to them, and the people who gave them worship were now too sick and weak to make sacrifice. Zeus therefore commanded Hades give Persephone back. The god of the Dead bowed to the will of almighty Zeus and agreed. He let Persephone go when Hermes arrived to take her back to the Land of the Living. But Hades first had played a trick on Persephone: he convinced her to eat three pomegranate seeds. Because Persephone had eaten the food of the Dead in the Land of the Dead, she was bound to that place for part of every year. When Persephone and her mother are reunited, the crops grow again, and the plants and trees are green, and the earth is warm and fertile. But every year for three months, Persephone goes back into the Underworld to live with Hades, one month for every pomegranate seed, and these are the months of winter when Persephone's absence makes Demeter sad, and the earth becomes cold and falls barren again for a time.

Part III

Demigods, Heroes, and Monsters

The Story of Perseus

Acrisius was king of Argos, and he had a beautiful daughter named Danae. But try as he might, he was unable to father a son. Acrisius asked an oracle what he needed to do to get a male heir, and the oracle replied by telling him that his daughter would bear a son, but the son would kill him. So Acrisius seized Danae and imprisoned her, thinking to prevent her from getting married and having children. But Father Zeus had seen Danae and desired her. One night Zeus came to Danae in the shape of a shower of gold. Danae found herself with child by him, and soon the child was born, a fine, strong boy. His mother gave him the name "Perseus."

When Acrisius found out that Danae had given birth to a son, he thought to rid himself of them both. He sealed mother and child into a chest and had the chest cast into the sea. The chest did not sink, but floated on the waves until it reached the island of Seriphus. A man named Dictys found the chest on the beach. He opened it and freed Danae and Perseus. Dictys took mother and son into his home, and he raised the boy as his own. Time passed, and Perseus grew into a fine figure of a man.

Now, Polydectes, the king of Seriphus and brother of Dictys, saw Danae and desired her, but he didn't dare touch her because Perseus was now a grown man and protected his mother. So Polydectes came up with a way to shame Perseus and get him out of the way so as to have Danae for himself. First Polydectes decided to throw a party to collect wedding gifts for his friend's daughter. Every guest was supposed to bring a gift of horses, but Perseus had no horses to give. Polydectes knew this, and he also knew that Perseus was honorable, brave, and strong, and these were things that could be used against him.

When Perseus appeared at the party, he apologized for not having horses to give. But he didn't want to dishonor either his host or the bridal couple, so he told Polydectes, "Name the gift, and I will get it for you."

Polydectes knew that the moment had come. This was what he could use to get rid of Perseus once and for all. He told Perseus to bring him back the head of Medusa, a woman who had once been beautiful but who had been raped by Poseidon in the temple of Athena. As punishment for desecrating her temple, Athena turned Medusa into a snake-haired creature so hideous that anyone who looked upon her face would instantly be turned into stone. After her transformation, Medusa was sent to live on an island in the Ethiopian Sea with the other Gorgons, who were the daughters of the Titans Ceto and Phorcys.

Before Perseus set out on his journey, Athena appeared to him, telling him he would first need to visit the Hesperides. They were the nymphs who lived at the very western edge of the world, tending a fantastic garden that held a tree that bore golden apples, which had been a wedding present from Hera to Zeus. Athena told Perseus the Hesperides would be able to help him defeat Medusa.

But first Perseus had to find the way to that divine garden, so he went in search of the Graeae, The Grey Ones. The Grey Ones were sisters of the Gorgons, three hideous old women who had but one eye they shared by passing it from one to the other. Perseus came to the cave of the Graeae. He watched the women passing the eye back and forth, taking turns using it to see. Perseus hid in a dark corner, and when the eye was being passed from one old hag to the next, he jumped out and snatched it away. The Graeae wailed and screamed at Perseus, but he held firm: they would get their eye back if they took him to the garden of the Hesperides. Finally, the women realized they had to do as Perseus asked, so they took him to the garden, and when they arrived there, Perseus gave them back their eye, as he had promised.

Perseus received many gifts to help him on his quest. From the Hesperides, he received a bag to put Medusa's head into. Zeus gave him a sword made of adamant. Hades gave him a cap that would make him invisible. Swift Hermes gave him winged sandals so he could fly, and a polished shield was Athena's gift.

Soon enough, Perseus arrived on the Gorgons' island. All about him were things that looked like statues, but really were the stone bodies of heroes who had tried to kill Medusa and failed. Because it was safe to look at Medusa's reflection, Perseus used the shiny inside of his shield as a mirror to guide him as he walked carefully towards the Gorgons' cave. Using the shield, he looked inside and saw Medusa and her sisters were sleeping. Like a flash, Perseus ran inside the cave. He took his sword of adamant and chopped off Medusa's head. The hair of snakes still writhing, Perseus stuffed the head into his bag. From the bleeding neck of the dead Gorgon leaped Pegasus, a great, winged horse, and Chrysaor, a beautiful young man. Pegasus and Chrysaor were the children of Medusa by Poseidon, and they were born when Perseus killed their mother. When the Gorgons realized Medusa was dead, they tried to chase Perseus, but because he was wearing the magical hat Hades had given him, they could not see him and thus could not catch him.

Perseus next headed towards Ethiopia, where King Cepheus and Queen Cassiopeia ruled. Now, Cassiopeia and Cepheus had a daughter of surpassing beauty, whose name was Andromeda. Cassiopeia boasted that Andromeda was more beautiful even than the most beautiful of the Nereids, the nymphs of the sea. This boast angered Poseidon, for his wife, Amphitrite, was herself a Nereid. Poseidon therefore commanded a great flood and sent a huge sea serpent to ravage the land all about. Cepheus went to the Oracle of Ammon to find out what to do. The oracle said that the floods would stop, and the monster would go away for good if Cepheus and Cassiopeia offered it their daughter. Cepheus and Cassiopeia were horrified by this, but the oracle had no further advice for them. Sacrificing Andromeda was the only way. Cepheus and Cassiopeia therefore took Andromeda and chained her to a rock next to the seashore. With many tears, they bid their beautiful daughter goodbye and then left her to her fate.

Flying with his winged sandals, Perseus approached the coast of Ethiopia, where he saw beautiful Andromeda chained to the rock. Perseus alighted next to her and asked what was wrong. Andromeda explained she was there as a sacrifice to Poseidon, that he might stop flooding the land and sending his monster to eat the people and their livestock. Perseus looked on Andromeda and felt pity for her and loved her. He told her he would help save the Ethiopians from the monster and save her too. He instructed her that once the monster appeared, she must keep her eyes closed and not look at any cost. Andromeda promised to do as he asked.

Perseus hid behind the rock and waited. Soon enough, the sea began to roil, and the waves began to rise: the monster was coming. But Perseus held fast. He waited until the monster was almost close enough to snatch Andromeda in its jaws, and then using his winged sandals he flew in between the princess and the beast. He plunged his hand into his special bag and drew out the head of Medusa. Being careful not to look at it himself, Perseus showed it to the sea serpent.

The serpent, being only a beast, did not have Perseus' wisdom, and so looked directly at the head. Even though Medusa was dead, her ugliness was still such that whatever looked at her turned to stone, and the sea monster was no different. The beast shuddered once and then fell into the water with a mighty splash. It sank to the bottom, a dead lump of monster-shaped stone.

Perseus freed Andromeda from her chains and brought her back to her baffled and exultant parents. Andromeda explained what Perseus had done, and the king and queen offered him Andromeda's hand in marriage. Perseus gladly accepted, and soon he and the princess were wed. Perseus and Andromeda returned to his birthplace in Argos as man and wife.

But Perseus had one last task to complete before he could settle in Argos. He returned to Seriphus to see his mother, where he found that Polydectes had continued to pursue her. Perseus vowed that Polydectes would molest Danae no more, so he went into the throne room and said, "Behold, Polydectes, here is the gift I promised!"

Perseus then took the head of Medusa out of the bag and showed it to Polydectes, who immediately turned into stone. As thanks for sheltering himself and his mother, Perseus made Dictys the king of Seriphus. Once this task was done, Perseus headed back home to Argos.

Acrisius learned that Perseus was on his way home. Acrisius was still worried about the prophecy that Danae's son would kill him, so he left Argos and went into exile in Thessaly. But this didn't save poor, greedy Acrisius. He decided to attend the funeral games that the king of Thessaly was holding after the death of his father. Unbeknownst to Acrisius, Perseus was among the competitors at throwing the discus. When it was Perseus' turn, he gave the discus a mighty throw, but it went astray and veered into the crowd where it struck Acrisius on the head, killing him instantly. Thus, the prophecy was fulfilled.

Although Perseus was now heir to the throne, he didn't want to become king by having killed Acrisius, so he gave the throne of Argos to Megapenthes, the son of Acrisius' brother Proetus. In exchange, Megapenthes gave Perseus the throne of Tiryns. Megapenthes also renounced any right to take revenge on Perseus for the death of his uncle.

When all his deeds were done and his throne secured, Perseus returned all the magical items he had received from the gods, with many thanks to their owners. The head of Medusa he gave as a special gift to Athena, who took it and fixed it into the aegis of Zeus, which she carried from time to time.

Perseus and Andromeda ruled wisely and well for the rest of their days, and when they died, Athena set them as constellations in the heavens next to Cepheus and Cassiopeia, and next to the great Pegasus, the winged horse of the gods.

The aegis of Zeus was often described in ancient times as a kind of shawl or wrap. Many representations of Athena show her wearing this, with the head of Medusa prominently displayed on it. Today, we still use the phrase "under the aegis" to indicate protection or legitimacy, because Zeus' aegis was a symbol of his royal power, which Athena might then wield as his proxy when she wore the aegis.

Heracles

Alcmene was a human woman married to a man called Amphitryon. While Amphitryon was away at war, Zeus looked upon Alcmene and wished to make love to her. Zeus took on the form of Amphitryon and went to Alcmene, who did not realize this was a god and not her husband. Alcmene became pregnant by Zeus.

Later that same night Amphitryon did come home from the war for real, and he also wanted to make love to his dear wife, whom he hadn't seen for a very long time. Alcmene welcomed him, and by

Amphitryon, she also became pregnant, the same night that she conceived a child by the god Zeus.

Now, Hera, the Queen of the Gods, knew Zeus had been unfaithful to her with Alcmene, and she was jealous of the child. Thinking to cause both the child and Zeus disgrace, when Alcmene went into labor she made a deal with Zeus that the first child born to the House of Perseus would become High King over the Greeks. Zeus agreed, and Hera contrived to delay the birth of Alcmene's twins while hastening the birth of Eurystheus, son of Sthenelus, who did become king when he was a man.

Alcmene gave her son by Zeus the name Heracles, perhaps thinking that by doing Hera this honor she would be appeased. The other twin was called Iphicles, whose son Iolaus became the great Heracles' charioteer.

But Alcmene suspected that naming the baby after Hera would not be enough to pacify the jealous goddess, so she exposed Heracles out on a hillside, to show that she did not want Zeus' child. Kind, grey-eyed Athena saw the baby, though, and saw this was her half-brother, who was destined to become a great hero. Athena, protectress of heroes, picked up the infant and brought him to Hera, who did not recognize him. Hera cooed over the infant, and played with him, and nursed him with milk from her breast, but Heracles sucked too hard, and it hurt her. Hera pushed the baby away, and a spray of milk came out of her breast. The milk went far into the heavens and became what we now call the Milky Way. But the milk did more than that: it gave Heracles many powers of strength and skill and strategy.

After Hera rejected the baby, Athena brought him back to his parents, who raised him. But Hera wasn't done trying to destroy this child: when Heracles and his brother were but toddlers, she sent poisonous serpents into their beds to bite them and kill them. Iphicles was afraid of the snakes and cried, but Heracles picked them up and strangled them. When his nurse came in to check on the boys, she found

Heracles waving the dead snakes about, playing with them as though they were toys.

Amphitryon was astounded by what his adopted son had done. He sent for the blind seer, Tiresias, and asked what the fate of Heracles would be. Tiresias, the great and wise prophet, said Heracles would become a hero who would defeat many monsters.

Thinking to make sure young Heracles had a proper education, Amphitryon hired a tutor named Linus to teach the boy. Now, Linus was a great poet and musician, famed throughout the land for the quality of his songs and verses. But Heracles was not a good student. He didn't care much for either songs or poetry, and one day he got frustrated with Linus hounding him to play the lyre properly. Heracles threw the lyre at Linus' head, striking him dead on the spot. Heracles was charged with murder, but he was acquitted based on the argument he had been defending himself against someone who was attacking him. Deciding it wasn't safe to have Heracles in his household, Amphitryon sent the young man out into the country to help look after his cattle.

Finally, Heracles decided it was time to go out into the world to seek his own path. But before he set out, he received a bow and arrows from Apollo, a sword from Hermes, armor from Hephaestus, and a robe from Athena, and for himself, he made a great club of wood. Thus armed, Heracles went to the city of Thebes, where he learned the Thebans were being forced to pay a high tribute to Erginus, king of the Minyans every year. Heracles didn't think this was fair, so he waited for the Minyan emissaries to show up to take the tribute home with them. When they arrived, Heracles attacked them. Heracles cut off their ears, noses, and hands, and tied these around the emissaries' necks, then sent them back to their king saying, "Tell Erginus that's all the tribute he is going to get."

Erginus, of course, was furious. He marshaled his army for an attack on Thebes, but Heracles helped the Thebans equip an army of their own, and when battle was joined great Heracles fought against the Minyans. Erginus and the Minyans were defeated, and as a reward, Creon, King of Thebes, gave his daughter Megara to be Heracles' wife.

Megara and Heracles were happily married for a time. Together they had two children, a son, and a daughter. But jealous Hera wasn't done with Heracles yet: she made him go mad, such that he killed both his children and his wife. But the madness wasn't permanent, and when Heracles came to himself, he was distraught. He loved his wife and children and couldn't believe he had killed them with his own hands. Determined to make amends for his crime, he went to the Oracle of Delphi to find out what he could do in penance. The Oracle told him the best thing he could do was to serve his cousin, King Eurystheus at his court in Tiryns. There Heracles was to do ten deeds that Eurystheus would command of him, and if he succeeded in those deeds, he would become immortal. Heracles didn't like the idea of becoming servant to Eurystheus, who had become king in Heracles place because of Hera's trick and who was weak and cowardly, but he also knew it was dangerous to refuse to follow the advice of the Oracle.

When Heracles arrived at Eurystheus' court, vowing to serve him in ten labors, Eurystheus couldn't believe his luck. Now he had a chance to bring this cousin of his down a peg, and maybe even get rid of him for good without having to do the dirty work himself. So Eurystheus thought of the most dangerous tasks possible and started giving them to Heracles.

The First Labor: The Nemean Lion

The first task was to vanquish the Nemean Lion. The Lion had been terrorizing the country around by kidnapping young women, and then when warriors came to rescue them, killing and eating the warriors. No one had been able to defeat the Lion because its hide was impenetrable. No ordinary mortal sword or arrow could pierce it, and the Lion's claws were so sharp and hard it could tear through even the hardest armor.

Heracles arrived in Nemea and went in search of the Lion. Soon enough, he spotted it, and the Lion saw him. The Lion stalked closer and closer, and Heracles, not knowing weapons could not pierce the beast's skin, fired arrows at it. The arrows bounced off the beast's hide, and still, it came towards Heracles. Heracles took up his club and began to swing it at the Lion. This didn't kill the Lion, but the beast didn't like it much and ran into a cave to hide. The cave had two mouths: Heracles blocked one and went into the other in search of the Lion.

Heracles entered the cave silently. He hefted his club, ready for the Lion's attack. Suddenly, the Lion shot out of the darkness straight towards Heracles. Heracles gave his club a mighty swing at the Lion's head, stunning it. Heracles dropped his weapons and ran over to the groggy beast. He grabbed it around the neck and squeezed with all his might until the Lion was dead.

As Heracles stood over the body of the dead Lion, he thought, "That hide can turn away any kind of weapon. I bet it would make the best armor."

So, he took out his knife and tried to skin the Lion but try as he might he couldn't pierce the animal's magical hide. Heracles was frustrated and about to give up, when grey-eyed Athena appeared to him and said, "Use one of the creature's own claws to skin it."

Heracles thanked the goddess and did as she suggested, and in no time, he had skinned the Lion, keeping the hide in one piece. The head of the Lion Heracles put on his head as a helmet, with the golden mane falling about his shoulders, and he used the skin of the forelegs to tie it about his neck, with the fearsome claws still attached at the ends.

Having completed the first task, Heracles marched back to Eurystheus' court, proudly wearing the lionskin. He strode into the throne room, saying, "See, Cousin? I have completed the first task. I wear the skin of the Nemean Lion."

But cowardly Eurystheus was so frightened by the lionskin he jumped into a nearby urn and ordered Heracles never to bring the evidence of his conquests into the city again, but rather to display them outside the walls. He also ordered Heracles not to come into the court precincts anymore: instead, he was to wait outside the city and Eurystheus would give him his next instructions there.

The Second Labor: The Lernean Hydra

The second task Eurystheus set Heracles was to slay the Lernean Hydra. The Hydra was a terrifying monster, the daughter of Typhon and Echidna, a swamp-dweller with nine heads, one of which was immortal, whose breath and blood was poisonous, and whom jealous Hera had raised specially to kill Heracles. Accompanied by his nephew, Iolaus, Heracles set out for the swamp, covering his mouth and nose with a cloth to protect himself from the Hydra's fumes.

Heracles and Iolaus arrived at the Hydra's lair, where Heracles fired a flaming arrow into the water. When the Hydra rose up out of the swamp to face this threat, Heracles struck at it with his mighty sword, slicing off one of its heads. Except in the place of the head that had just fallen, two more sprang up. Heracles tried again, but the same thing happened.

Heracles called out to his nephew for help. Iolaus thought quickly and then ran to kindle fire. He took a flaming torch in his hand and said, "Uncle, slice off the creature's heads, and I will seal the wounds with the torch."

Working together, Heracles and Iolaus attacked one head after another, Heracles slicing it off with his mighty sword and Iolaus plunging the torch into the wound so another head couldn't grow back in its place. But as they were getting ready to fight the last, immortal head, Hera saw they were winning and sent a huge crab to distract

Heracles. The crab nipped at Heracles' heels with its claws, but the great hero paid it no mind: he stomped on the crab and crushed it, then went about chopping off the remaining, immortal head, and the Hydra was dead. Heracles took the remaining, immortal head, which was still alive and moving, and placed it under a huge rock. He also dipped his arrow points into the creature's poisonous blood. Hera, meanwhile, upset that the hero had killed two of her pets, took the Hydra and the crab and placed them in the heavens as the constellations Hydra and Cancer.

Heracles and Iolaus went back to Eurystheus in triumph. Disappointed that Heracles had been successful and, worse still, was still alive, Eurystheus warned that tasks would only get harder from here. He also said that killing the Hydra wouldn't count towards his ten tasks, since Iolaus had helped slay the creature.

The Third Labor: The Ceryneian Hind

The next thing the wretched king demanded Heracles do was to capture the Ceryneian Hind, a golden-antlered deer so fast that it could outrun an arrow. Now, the Hind itself wasn't dangerous like the Lion or the Hydra had been, but it was an animal sacred to Artemis, goddess of the hunt. Eurystheus was hoping that if Heracles caught it, that Artemis would punish him, and that would finally be the end of the hero.

Heracles set out on the hunt for the Hind. He looked up and down and here and there, and finally one morning as he was awaking he saw a flash across the meadow. It was the shine of the Hind's golden antlers. Swift Heracles ran towards the Hind, but even he wasn't fast enough to catch it. He chased the animal all through Greece; he ran after it all through Thrace; the Hind eluded him through Istria and the land of the Hyperboreans. Heracles pursued the Hind for a full year, but never could he get close enough even to touch it.

Finally, the Hind began to tire, and it lay down to sleep. Heracles saw this and wove a soft net. He threw the net over the sleeping Hind, and thus captured it. He put a leash around the Hind's neck and began to lead it back to Eurystheus' court. But Heracles knew this was an animal sacred to Artemis, so as soon as he chanced upon one of her temples, he stopped and prayed to her, explaining why he had the Hind, and that it was part of a penance assigned by the Oracle at Delphi. He promised he would set the animal free as soon as he had shown it to Eurystheus. Artemis appeared to Heracles and listened to his prayer. She agreed to let him show the Hind to the king, as long as he set it free immediately afterward. Heracles thanked the goddess and set out for Tiryns.

When Heracles arrived at Tiryns, he called for Eurystheus to come and see the wonderful Hind. Eurystheus looked down upon the hero and the animal from atop the city walls, then told Heracles, "Bring the animal inside the city and put it in the menagerie with my other beasts."

But Heracles knew he couldn't do that: he had made a promise to swift Artemis that he would let the Hind go. So, he took the leash off the Hind's neck, whereupon it immediately bounded away. Heracles shouted to Eurystheus, "If you want this animal for your zoo, you will have to catch it yourself."

The Fourth Labor: The Erymanthian Boar

Eurystheus was furious that Heracles had let the Hind go, and that he had been so successful in each of the dangerous tasks he had been set. So, he thought and finally decided to send Heracles on an adventure that would be the most dangerous yet: to capture the Erymanthian boar and bring it back to Tiryns, alive. Now, the boar was a fearsome beast, huge, strong, and old, with tusks as long and as sharp as sabers. No hunter who had encountered it had ever returned from the hunt alive. Eurystheus thought that surely this task would be the end of the great hero.

Heracles put on his lionskin cloak and took up his weapons, and headed for Mount Erymanthos, a place that was home to many wild beasts, including the boar. On the way, he stopped to visit the centaur Pholus, who was an old friend of his. Pholus offered the hero dinner, and when Heracles asked for wine Pholus at first refused. He only had one jar, and it had been a gift from Dionysus himself. What was more, if he opened it, the smell would attract other centaurs. Heracles convinced Pholus to open it anyway, and sure enough, all the centaurs from the neighborhood round showed up asking for a drink. But they forgot to water down the wine, and soon they were all quite drunk.

Now, a drunk centaur is a nasty centaur, and they soon started attacking Heracles. Heracles didn't want to hurt Pholus' friends, but he had no choice. He shot at them with his arrows he had dipped in the blood of the Hydra. The ones that he hit dropped dead on the spot; the others ran away toward the cave of Chiron, the greatest of the centaurs.

As Heracles was firing at the retreating centaurs, one of the arrows accidentally hit Chiron, who hadn't been at the party and who hadn't been attacking Heracles. Heracles was devastated at this. He pulled out the arrow and put on some medicine that Chiron told him to use, but it was no use. Some say Chiron soon died of the wound; others say that he was immortal, but the pain from the poison was so great that he offered up his immortality in exchange for Prometheus' freedom, and that Heracles set the Fire-Bringer free after this.

Pholus was curious as to how Heracles had been able to kill the others so quickly, so he picked up an arrow. He wasn't careful with it, though, and ended up pricking his skin with it, poisoning himself as well.

Once Heracles managed to get free of the rampaging centaurs, he continued his hunt for the boar. He found the animal on a mountainside, but it eluded him. Heracles chased it for some days but couldn't subdue it until he was finally able to drive it into a deep bank of snow. The boar became stuck in the snow, and Heracles was able to throw a net over it and capture it. Heracles put the great boar on his mighty shoulders and marched back to Tiryns in triumph. When he arrived, he shouted for Eurystheus to come and see his catch. Eurystheus came to the city walls, where he took one look at the boar. The beast was so terrifying to him that cowardly Eurystheus ran away and hid.

The Fifth Labor: The Augean Stables

King Augeas was a ruler wealthy in cattle. He had so many animals it was impossible to keep the stables clean. Eurystheus thought that maybe he could defeat the great Heracles not by pitting him against monsters, but by making him clean up mountains of dung, a humiliating task for a mighty warrior.

Heracles went to Elis, where Augeas was king. Without mentioning that he was there at Eurystheus' bidding, Heracles told the king, "I can cleanse your stables in one day if you will pay me a portion of your herds."

Augeas was surprised that anyone would offer to clean the stables at all, never mind boast they could do it in a single day, so he accepted Heracles' offer. Heracles then had all the animals moved out to pasture. Then he went and diverted the courses of two rivers, the Alpheus and Peneus so they flowed down and through the cattle-sheds, sweeping away all the dung in one powerful surge. When the sheds were clean, Heracles put the rivers back into their beds.

Augeas was astounded. But when he learned that Heracles had done this at Eurystheus' command as part of his penance, he refused to pay. Augeas agreed to submit to arbitration over the dispute, but when his son Phyleus came forth saying that Augeas had indeed made a deal with Heracles to pay him, Augeas forced Heracles and Phyleus to leave the country. Heracles eventually went to war with Augeas to exact payment. After defeating Augeas' army and killing the king and sacking the city, Heracles put honest Phyleus on the throne. In gratitude for his victory, Heracles competed in Olympian games at Elis and founded twelve altars to the immortal gods there.

Heracles returned to Tiryns to let Eurystheus know the task had been completed. But word had come to Eurystheus that Heracles had demanded payment for it, and so Eurystheus said that cleansing the stables would not count among the ten tasks Heracles was required to perform.

The Sixth Labor: The Stymphalian Birds

On the shores of Lake Stymphalis was a large wood in which a great flock of birds had made their nests. Now, these were no ordinary birds: if any human walked near or through those woods, the birds would set upon them and eat them alive. The people who lived near the lake were in constant fear of these flesh-eating birds. Eurystheus decided that ridding the country of those birds would be the next task for the great Heracles.

Heracles arrived at Lake Stymphalis. He wasn't worried about being set upon by the birds himself since there was no way they could pierce his lion-skin armor. But he was puzzled about how to get rid of so many creatures. As Heracles sat and thought, grey-eyed Athena appeared to him. She gave him a rattle of bronze made by skilled Hephaestus, and this was the very thing Heracles needed.

Heracles used the rattle to make a thunderous racket that startled the birds from their trees. As soon as the birds took flight, Heracles put down the rattle, then took up his bow and shot the birds from the sky. Heracles went all the way around the wood, putting up the birds and then bringing them down, one by one. Soon all the birds were dead, and the people of the lake were free from their terror.

The Seventh Labor: The Cretan Bull

Asterius, king of Crete, had died without an heir, and Minos wished to ascend the throne. To convince the people of his right to be king, Minos said he had the favor of the gods and that they would give him whatever he prayed for. So, Minos made sacrifice to Poseidon and prayed for a great Bull to come up out of the sea, promising that if Poseidon answered his prayer, he would then immediately sacrifice the animal. Poseidon heard Minos and sent a great Bull of surpassing size and beauty out of the sea. The people of Crete then agreed that Minos had the favor of the gods and made him their king. But Minos did not keep his promise to Poseidon: The Bull was too beautiful to sacrifice, he thought, and so he put it amongst his herds and sacrificed another in its stead.

This angered Poseidon greatly. He therefore cursed Pasiphae, Minos' wife and queen of Crete, with an unquenchable lust for the Bull. She went to Daedalus, the clever builder, and told him to make a hollow statue in the shape of a cow, one the Bull of Poseidon could not possibly resist. Daedalus did the queen's bidding, and she hid within the Bull. Soon enough, the Bull came and mated with what he thought was a fine cow, but really it was Pasiphae inside the statue he was coupling with. Soon Pasiphae found herself pregnant by the Bull. The son she bore had the head of a bull and the body of a man, and it was called the Minotaur. Minos imprisoned it in the labyrinth, which was also built by Daedalus, where it lived until it was killed by the hero Theseus, whose tale shall be told later.

Eurystheus decided that sending Heracles to capture the Cretan Bull would be his next command, for Poseidon had made the animal untamable as part of his revenge for Minos not making it into a sacrifice. Heracles arrived at Crete and explained to King Minos what he wanted. Minos said he was welcome to take the Bull, but that Heracles would have to capture it himself; neither Minos nor any of his men would help with that task because the Bull was too dangerous.

Heracles soon captured the Bull and brought it back to show Eurystheus. The beast was too fearsome for the king's menagerie, so Heracles let it go loose. It roamed through Sparta and Arcadia until it came to Marathon, where it laid waste to the countryside until the hero Theseus killed it.

The Eighth Labor: The Mares of Diomedes

The Mares of Diomedes were a gift to King Diomedes from the war god, Ares, and were ferocious horses so savage they refused to eat grass and grain as their common cousins did. Instead, they had been taught to eat human flesh. Word of these horses came to Eurystheus. If monsters and man-eating lions had not been enough to bring down the great hero, perhaps flesh-eating horses would do the trick. Eurystheus therefore told Heracles to go and bring back the Mares of Diomedes.

Heracles went to the stables where the horses were kept. There he attacked Diomedes and fed him to his horses. Once they had devoured their master, the horses became docile and never again desired to eat flesh. Heracles brought the horses back to Tiryns, where Eurystheus dedicated the horses to the great goddess Hera.

The Ninth Labor: The Belt of Hippolyta

Word of Heracles' successes had spread throughout all of Tiryns. Everyone followed his exploits and waited for news of what new deed he would perform. The royal family was no exception to this, and one day Eurystheus' daughter came to her father and said, "Please, father, may I set the next task? Have mighty Heracles fetch the belt of Hippolyta, queen of the Amazons, for I wish to have it for my own."

Eurystheus granted his daughter's request and told Heracles that he must bring back the belt of Hippolyta.

Heracles went to the city of Themiscyra, on the banks of the Thermidon River, where the Amazons lived. The Amazons were a race of women warriors, trained in battle, who cut off their right breasts so they would be unhindered when using their weapons. Their left breasts they kept so they could nurse their infants. So skilled and courageous were these warriors that they were beloved of Ares. Hippolyta, their queen, was far and away above the others in her prowess, such that Ares had given her a belt as a token of his esteem, and it was this belt that Heracles had been sent to fetch.

Heracles went before Hippolyta and explained his errand. Hippolyta ignored him, and instead sent her Amazons to fight with Heracles. The Amazons were strong and swift, and cunning with their weapons, but Heracles was mightier still, and soon he had defeated them all. Last he fought with Queen Hippolyta. It was a ferocious battle, but in the end, Heracles killed the powerful queen and took her belt, which he brought back to Eurystheus.

The Tenth Labor: The Cattle of Geryon

The tenth deed Eurystheus commanded Heracles to do was to bring back the cattle of Geryon. These were fine, beautiful cattle, whose coats turned red when touched by the light of the sun. Now, a herd of cattle might not seem to be such a terrifying foe, but it wasn't the animals who were the dangerous part of this task. No, indeed, to get to the cattle, first Heracles would have to get past the cowherd, Eurytion, and his two-headed dog, Orthus. These might not seem so daunting, either, after Heracles' adventures with the Hydra and the Nemean Lion. But Geryon himself was not to be trifled with. The son of Chrysaor, he who had sprung from the neck of Medusa, and of the Oceanid Callirhoe, Geryon was a three-bodied giant who had four wings. He was a vicious warrior, terrifically strong, and ferociously guarded his cattle.

Geryon and his herds lived on the island of Erytheia, a far place in the most distant reaches of Oceanus, the encircling sea. The first problem Heracles had to solve was how to get there. Heracles walked across the breadth of Europe and coming to the end of the Iberian

Peninsula he set up two pillars, one at the tip of Iberia and another across the straits in Libya, as markers of his journey, on which he had many other adventures not told here. The sun was hot in Iberia, so much so that Heracles was feeling angry about it, so he nocked an arrow to his bowstring and pointed it at the sun in his irritation. Helios, the Sun god, was so surprised and amused by Heracles' presumption that he loaned the hero a boat that would take him to Erytheia.

When Heracles arrived on Erytheia, he first slew Eurytion and Orthus. Then he had a long and difficult battle with Geryon, who had the advantage of six arms and three heads, not to mention he was a giant and much bigger than Heracles. But soon Heracles defeated Geryon too. He loaded the cattle into the boat the Sun had lent him, and sailed back first to Tartessus, where he returned the boat to Helios. After this, Heracles drove the cattle back to Tiryns, completing his tenth deed at the command of King Eurystheus.

The Eleventh Labor: The Golden Apples of the Hesperides

Now, Heracles had worked for King Eurystheus for eight years and one month and had completed the ten deeds the oracle had demanded, but Eurystheus still wasn't satisfied, and he refused to let Heracles leave his service. Eurystheus declared that killing the Lernean Hydra and cleansing the Augean Stables hadn't counted, because in the first instance Heracles had help, and in the second he had demanded payment. So Eurystheus told Heracles he had to perform two additional deeds, the first of which was to fetch golden apples from the garden of the Hesperides.

The tree that grew the golden apples had been a wedding gift from mighty Zeus to Hera. This tree she put in a garden at the end of the world, and it was guarded by a great dragon, and by the Hesperides, nymphs who were the daughters of the great Titan, Atlas. Their garden was at the very end of the world, and no hero had ever been able to get past the dragon to take the apples.

Some say that Heracles made his way to the garden and killed the dragon with arrows dipped in the poisonous blood of the Hydra, but others say he obtained the apples using a trick he had learned from Prometheus, and this is how that came about. The garden of the Hesperides was at the edge of the world, near where the Titan Atlas held up the sky. Heracles knew the Hesperides likely would allow Atlas to take some apples since he was their father. So, Heracles strode up to Atlas and said, "I would like some apples from the tree in your daughters' garden, and in exchange, I will hold up the sky for you while you are away."

Atlas agreed and shifted the burden of the sky onto great Heracles' shoulders. It was a heavy burden to bear. Heracles soon felt that he could not hold it up for much longer. But then the Titan Atlas reappeared, carrying three apples. Atlas looked at Heracles and said, "I think you are doing a fine job of holding up the sky. There's really no need for me to take it back."

Heracles nearly panicked. He did not want to be stuck holding up the sky forever. But then he thought of a way to trick Atlas into taking the sky back. Heracles said, "I can keep holding the sky for you, but it's cutting into my shoulders. Can you take it back for a while so that I can find some padding?"

Atlas agreed to take the sky back on his shoulders, whereupon Heracles snatched up the apples that the Titan had placed on the ground and left the garden of the Hesperides, never to return. And poor Atlas still stands under the weight of the sky, which he cannot put down.

The Twelfth Labor: Cerberus, Dog of the Underworld

Heracles returned to Tiryns bearing the golden apples. Upon his return King Eurystheus set him one final task, thinking that maybe this would be the one that would finish off the great hero. Eurystheus told Heracles that he had to bring back Cerberus, the three-headed dog who guarded the gates to the Underworld.

Heracles marched into the Underworld and went before Hades. He asked the dreaded god whether he might borrow Cerberus because this was the final task he had to perform to satisfy the oracle and leave the service of Eurystheus. Hades agreed on one condition: Heracles had to subdue the dog without using any weapons.

Now, Cerberus not only had three heads: he also had a serpent for a tail. Heracles therefore would have to protect himself from sharp teeth at not one, but two ends of the giant animal. Covering himself in the thick hide of the Nemean Lion, Heracles went in search of Cerberus. The hero found the great hound at the gates of Acheron, one of the five rivers that flowed through the Underworld. Mindful of his agreement with Hades, Heracles approached Cerberus empty-handed. He leaped upon the great dog and put his arms around its throat. Cerberus struck at mighty Heracles with its serpent's tail, but the serpent could not bite through the lionskin. Heracles squeezed and squeezed, and soon Cerberus was cowed by the chokehold.

Heracles returned to Tiryns, the great hound at his heels. He showed the dreadful creature to King Eurystheus, who declared Heracles' penance done, and released him from his service. And as he promised, Heracles brought Cerberus back to Hades.

The great Heracles had many other adventures that have not been told here. Heracles fought with monsters, helped on quests, and did many heroic deeds before he died and was placed among the stars by the eternal gods.

Theseus and the Minotaur

Aegeus was king of Athens, and his friend Pittheus was king of Troezen. Aegeus had no heir to his throne, so he consulted the Delphic Oracle about what to do. The oracle said something confusing: it seemed to indicate that Aegeus shouldn't drink any wine until he got to Athens. Wanting to make sure he understood the oracle, he went to Troezen for advice. Aegeus told Pittheus what the prophecy was. Pittheus understood it and told Aegeus he should not make love to a woman until he returned home to Athens. Pittheus had a daughter named Aethra, and he convinced Aegeus to take her back to Athens with him and take her into his bed when he got home.

Soon enough, Aethra became pregnant by Aegeus and gave birth to a son whom she called Theseus. Aegeus decided he would set a task for the child to do when he had grown into a man, a task that would prove him worthy to be king of Athens when Aegeus was gone. So, Aegeus buried a sword and a pair of sandals beneath a great rock. He told only Aethra that he had done this so that only Theseus would know where to look.

Theseus grew into a young man, tall and strong, and skilled with all kinds of weapons. His mother told him about the rock with the sword and sandals underneath it. Theseus decided the time had come for him to seek his fortune in the world and to take up his inheritance, so he went to the rock and, putting his mighty shoulder to it, pushed it aside. He took up the sandals and the sword and set out for Athens. Theseus had many great adventures on his way to Athens.

When Theseus arrived at Athens, he found that the sorceress Medea had become consort to King Aegeus, his father, and had been trying to help him get more children. Medea realized who Theseus was, but Aegeus did not. Medea feared Theseus and convinced Aegeus he was an enemy. Medea told Aegeus to invite Theseus to a banquet and there give him a cup of poison in place of wine. Aegeus agreed to this.

Theseus went to the banquet as Aegeus' guest, and the cup of poison was put before him, but Theseus did not drink of it just then. When the meat was passed at the table, Theseus drew the sword that he had taken from beneath the rock, as though he were going to use it to cut some meat for himself. Aegeus saw him do this and, recognizing the sword, grabbed the cup of poison and dumped it out, and welcomed Theseus into his household as his son and heir.

Making Theseus heir to the throne of Athens did not sit well with the sons of Pallas, who also dwelled in Athens and who had thought the throne should be theirs when Aegeus died. The sons of Pallas, therefore, went to war against Aegeus, and they set up an ambush against Theseus and his men. But a herald of the Pallantides saw this and told Theseus what was waiting up ahead. Theseus and his men, therefore, were ready when the ambush came, and they defeated the Pallantides, who were all killed or scattered.

Theseus went back to Athens with a will to making himself useful and beloved of the people. The very first thing he did was to deal with the Cretan Bull that Heracles had loosed on the countryside. The people were grateful to Theseus: The Bull had been destroying their fields and orchards, and no one had been able to kill it or make it go away. Mighty Theseus captured the Bull and sacrificed it to the eternal gods.

Besides the Cretan Bull, the Athenians had one other very great sorrow. Many years ago, Androgeus, son of Minos, king of Crete, had come to Athens to participate in athletic contests. But Androgeus never went home again: some say he went out to try his luck against the Cretan Bull and was killed by it; others say that Aegeus feared he might support the Pallantides against him and so assassinated him. Whatever the cause of Androgeus' death, Minos went to Athens to demand satisfaction, but Aegeus would not hear him. Therefore, Minos declared war on the Athenians, and since his cause was just the gods sided with Minos and brought drought and famine along with the destruction of war.

In desperation, the Athenians prayed to Zeus and asked what they could do to end their suffering. Zeus told them to give Minos whatever he asked of them. Minos demanded that every nine years Athens should send a tribute of seven youths and seven maidens to Crete. The Athenians agreed, and this brought an end to the war, drought, and famine. But the tribute was the beginning of another kind of suffering. Minos took those young people and locked them in the Labyrinth, a winding, confusing maze of tunnels and walls in which dwelt the Minotaur, half-man, half-bull, who feasted on the flesh of those who lost themselves within his maze. The agreement with the Athenians said that Minos could do this as long as the Minotaur should live.

Soon after Theseus arrived in Athens, it came time for the tribute of young people to be sent to Crete once more. Theseus arranged it so he would be among the youths of the tribute, for he thought he might be able to kill the Minotaur and thus bring an end to the tribute once and for all. The young people were supposed to be unarmed, but Theseus managed to hide a sword in his clothing. In token of the mourning of the people of Athens for the young men and women who were being sent to their awful fate, the Athenian ship sailed out to Crete with black sails. Aegeus hoped Theseus would make good his promise and come back alive, and he wanted to know as soon as possible what the outcome of his adventure had been. He made an agreement with the ship's captain that when the ship returned to Athens, it should have white sails if all was well, or black sails if Theseus had failed and was dead.

The ship set sail for Crete. When it arrived, Minos and the royal household and the people of the city came to see the new tribute that had been sent to feed the Minotaur. Ariadne, the daughter of Minos, looked upon Theseus and, seeing that he was an unusually handsome young man, fell in love with him. Ariadne determined to help Theseus and so went to him bearing a ball of thread. Ariadne told Theseus to affix the thread to the gate of the Labyrinth and to unspool it as he walked through the maze. To find his way out, Theseus had only to follow the clew back to the entrance.

Theseus thanked Ariadne. He bid the other young people wait for him near the entrance of the Labyrinth, then did as Ariadne instructed, reeling out the thread as he proceeded through the maze. After what seemed like days, Theseus came to the center of the Labyrinth. There stood the Minotaur, a huge beast with massive horns. Only the head was that of a bull; the rest of the body was that of a man, thick and muscular. The Minotaur charged at Theseus, and there was a fierce battle. In the end, Theseus was the victor, and the Minotaur lay dead.

Following the thread, he had spooled out, Theseus returned to the entrance of the Labyrinth. Gathering up the young people, he shepherded them back to the harbor. Ariadne had also been waiting outside the Labyrinth, anxious to see whether Theseus would survive. She asked Theseus to take her with him, and he agreed. Some say that Theseus and his friends escaped by putting holes in all the Cretan ships so they could not follow him, but, however it came about, the Athenians could escape without being harried by the Cretans.

It was a long journey back to Athens. One night, the young people stopped on the island of Naxos to rest. While they were sleeping, the god Dionysus came and looked upon Ariadne. He fell in love with her and carried her away to be his bride. When Theseus and the others awoke in the morning, they saw that Ariadne was gone. They called and searched for her, but she was nowhere to be found. With heavy hearts, they got back on board their ship and set sail for Athens.

Between the rush to escape from Minos and their grief at the disappearance of Ariadne, the Athenians forgot to change the sails on their ship. Now, Aegeus had stood on the Acropolis every day since Theseus' departure, keeping a lookout for the return of his son, and when he spied the returning ship and its black sails, he cast himself down from the rock in despair, thinking that Theseus was dead, and so perished.

Theseus arrived at a city in confusion. Some were in mourning over the death of Aegeus, others were rejoicing at the return of Theseus and were eager to crown him king. But before taking the throne, Theseus made sure that the proper sacrifices and rituals were performed for Aegeus. And when he finally did become king, Theseus made many wise laws and helped to strengthen the city in many ways.

The image of the Labyrinth and the Minotaur had a lasting effect on European culture, extending even to medieval Christian sacred architecture. Craig Wright notes that the labyrinths that decorate the floors of many French cathedrals once held the image not of Christ or other Christian symbol but of the Minotaur. Wright says the Minotaur likely was a symbol for the Devil and that the progress into and out of the cathedral labyrinth was meant to symbolize Christ going into Hell to free the souls there between his crucifixion and resurrection.

Preview of Roman Mythology

A Captivating Guide to Roman Gods, Goddesses, and Mythological Creatures

Introduction

Gravitas was a founding principle of Roman society. Life can be brutal, and the Romans figured out early that guiding one's actions with weightiness or seriousness—or, in today's word—intentionality—was necessary. Using *gravitas* as a guide for life made them exceptionally practical—although not particularly creative. In fact, the Romans were an unimaginative society. The creativity they did employ was greatly borrowed –sometimes forcibly--from other cultures.

Only a few of their gods were entirely Roman. Because little is written during the early years of Rome, it is difficult to separate their own divinities as opposed to those they appropriated.

Originally, the Romans were farmers. Many of their earliest gods dealt with crops, rain, and their main river—the Tiber.

Gravitas, with its intentionality and practicality, led the Romans to think affinities could be cultivated by making their gods look like those of their neighbors. These affinities made assimilation or conquest much easier. Allowing citizens to keep their religious traditions, a widespread practice among some early civilizations, helped make them more compliant with Roman rule. And if Roman traditions looked like the traditions of the conquered peoples, the subjugated populace would believe they truly belonged to Rome.

Like a modern exercise in building a commercial brand, Roman writers of the first century BC developed stories of Roman myth and history to manufacture legitimacy for their rulers. Virgil (70–19 BC), for instance, gave Rome its most important work of authority—the *Aeneid*, which told the story of Rome's roots in the Trojan War; they were descended from Trojans, the enemies of the Greeks. We'll take a brief look at the truth of this possibility in "Chapter 4 — Borrowings from Etruria."

The Shape of Things to Come

We will look at many aspects of the Roman gods, goddesses, and mythological creatures. Each of the first six chapters begins with a narrative scene which helps bring the legendary and mythical characters to life.

In chapter 1, we explore the seeds of legitimacy that Virgil planted regarding the Trojan connection to Rome. Though Aeneas was a minor character in Homer's epic *Iliad*, Virgil shows Aeneas to be the epitome of what a good Roman should be—heroic, serious, virtuous, and devoted. And, important to the *Iliad*, Aeneas was one of the sons of Venus or, as she was known to the Greeks, Aphrodite—the goddess of love.

How do we get from a Trojan demigod to the reality of Rome? This is the topic of chapter 2. In this chapter, we explore the foundation of that great city by the semi-divine, wolf-suckled brothers, Romulus and Remus. We also consider the myth of Aeneas's son, Ascanius, who was also known as Iulus—the basis of the name of Julius, and the basis of the Julio-Claudian dynasty of the Roman Empire. Virgil gave the family of Julius Caesar its back-story to make his patron, and Rome's first emperor, Augustus, seem worthier of being a living god.

In chapter 3, we examine the gods of Roman origin as well as Roman mythological creatures.

Chapter 4 focuses on the Etruscan influence on Roman mythology. Latin culture co-opted Minerva as its own, and then gave her the Greek attributes of the goddess Athena.

Perhaps the strongest influence in Roman mythology came from the Greeks. The Greeks were far more creative, and their legends were far richer and more detailed. The Greek influence is the topic of chapter 5. The Greeks had expanded their influence to the southern portion of the Italian peninsula far from the tiny Kingdom of Rome. In the centuries before the Roman Republic, the Greeks had expanded into southern France and eastern Spain.

In chapter 6, we delve into the world of Celtic influence and see how the gods of the Celts were melded with the Roman pantheon in creative ways. What we know about the Celtic pantheon comes from the Romans. The Celts used oral storytelling to record their history for generations.

Finally, in chapter 7, we take a brief look at the potential truths behind the Roman gods, goddesses, and creatures. Every myth had a beginning, and in this chapter, we explore some of the possibilities.

The Romans were builders and innovators in many industries. They took existing resources and shaped them to suit their needs. But they also adopted the creative ideas of others. Over time, the Roman pantheon became increasingly a melting pot of ideas blended into a cultural potpourri.

Chapter 1 — The Trojan Connection

Goddess Juno—Jupiter's queen—looked down upon the ragtag fleet of Trojan ships, led by Aeneas, and she sneered with delight as she thought of sinking them to the bottom of the sea. Juno despised Troy and its people. Petty and immature, like all the gods and goddesses—they lacked the maturity and humility to act wisely.

She hated Troy because of Paris, Prince of Troy, snubbed Juno when he judged who was the most beautiful goddess—between Juno (the Greek Hera), Minerva (Athena) and Venus (Aphrodite).

The dispute began at the wedding of the Greek goddess, Thetis, to King Peleus of Aegina.

One goddess, though, despised the event. Eris, goddess of discord, and daughter of Jupiter and Juno was not being invited because the other gods wanted a peaceful event. Her exclusion angered her. She said, "to the fairest one" and threw a golden apple over the wall and into the party. No one caught the apple, but three goddesses claimed the golden apple as her own—Juno, Minerva, and Venus. To settle the dispute, they asked Jupiter to judge between them.

Understanding the potentially dire consequences of such a task, Jupiter chose a mortal to judge who should own the apple based on the inscription: "to the fairest one." That mortal was the fair-minded Paris, Prince of Troy. Jupiter understandably protected himself by choosing Paris, since the choice would upset the two goddesses not selected—and that hostility might last forever. Jupiter protected his own sanity and safety by transferring the dangerous duty onto an expendable and convenient mortal. Perhaps even wise Minerva did not realize how truly foolish Paris would be to accept such an inherently dangerous task.

After the wedding celebration was over Mercury (Hermes) escorted the three goddesses to Asia Minor—also known as Anatolia, or modern Turkey. There, they bathed in a local spring on Mount Ida, not very far from Troy. After freshening up, they found Paris, sitting on a log under the shade of a mature tree, tending to his flock on the slopes of the mountain. Naturally, the prince was surprised to have the three lovely goddesses present him with this interesting challenge.

At first, the goddesses posed before the honest prince--Juno, Minerva and finally Venus. But Paris could not decide.

"I'm afraid, my ladies," he said, taking a deep breath before continuing, "that this is an impossible task. You are each incredibly beautiful, and my mind is at an impasse."

"What if we were to show you our full form," asked Venus, "without the visual impediment of the divine clothing we typically wear out of sensible modesty?"

The other two goddesses nodded encouragingly.

Paris smiled. He had seen naked women before and knew the pleasure that came with the sight. In fact, his wife was the beautiful mountain nymph, Oenone. The thought that three major goddesses would willingly bare themselves for his judgment aroused him more than he thought possible.

He spoke cautiously, though. He knew of their power, and he did not want to answer rashly and risk offending any of them.

"I can sense the importance of this challenge you've given me. If it pleases each of you that I—a mere mortal—view your beauty in its entirety to complete the charge you've laid upon me, then I will humbly do this thing as you request. I sincerely hope that this will be enough to settle in my own mind an answer to your question."

Again, Juno went first because of her seniority amongst the three goddesses. Quietly, she unfastened her garment and let it fall to her feet. Slowly, she stepped out of it and moved toward the young man as he remained seated.

Closer she came, slowly advancing. When she was close enough to touch, she showed the young man her neck and breasts down to her abdomen. She showed him her thighs and buttocks, as well as the small of her back. As she displayed her physical form in all its splendor, she whispered to him, bribing him in exchange for his vote for her. She would give him rule over all of Europe and Asia, and not merely Asia Minor—from Eriu to Yamato—Ireland to Japan.

As Juno returned to her clothes, the other two goddesses guessed what she had done. Each secretly decided to sway the young prince's decision with the best possible bribe they could consider.

Next, Minerva dropped her clothing and approached Paris, equally seductively. Because of her temperament as a warrior and protectress of the homeland, her movements added power and finesse which Juno lacked. Her earthiness left Paris breathless. As Minerva displayed up-close each curve of her beautiful body, she whispered to him that she could make the young prince the wisest and most skilled of all mortals in the art of war. All he would need to do was to choose her as the owner of the golden apple.

Moments later, as Minerva restored her vestments, Venus dropped her gown and stepped forward, turning with a coy seduction that left the young mortal's heart pounding with each step. This was the goddess of love and Paris felt once again the impossibility of this challenge.

Venus promised that if Paris chose her, she would make it possible for him to marry the most beautiful mortal woman in all the world—the already married, Helen, wife of King Menelaus of Sparta.

Assailed by so much feminine charm, the bribe which raked most heavily across his mind was the one that most closely matched the feelings overpowering his mind, body, and soul. Helplessly, he chose Venus and thus sealed the fate of Troy, setting in motion events that would eventually lead to the creation of Rome.

When Helen left her husband to join Paris in Troy, the Greeks banded together to attack the Trojan capital. Why would there be such unity amongst the usually conflicting Greek city-states? The leaders of those city-states had agreed to that attack.

Helen was so beautiful that almost every king in the Greek kingdoms sought her hand in marriage. Her wise father feared any man he chose for his daughter would soon lose her because the others would continue to fight over her, even after she married. Minerva's wisdom guided him to bind each king to the father's decision by swearing to protect Helen's marriage to whomever she was to be pledged. Only after each king gave his pledge did the father reveal his choice.

Thus, when Helen left her husband, the other Greek kings were duty-bound to go after her—to protect her marriage to Menelaus of Sparta. For a decade, they laid siege to Troy to protect those wedding vows between Menelaus and Helen. In the end, Troy lost, and the city was destroyed.

Now that Juno and Minerva had ensured the collapse of Troy, after its ten-year war against the Greeks, its remaining citizens were dispersed throughout the eastern Mediterranean. The future heritage of Troy depended upon Aeneas, second cousin of the now dead princes of Troy—including Hector, Paris, Deiphobus, Polydorus.

Juno despised Troy for several reasons.

From her great height, Juno also looked down upon her favorite city—Carthage—and dreaded the thought the descendants of Aeneas would someday ruin the now-fledgling town. If only she could stop Aeneas and end the prophecy concerning him.

Juno also despised the Trojans because her own daughter, Hebe, had been replaced as Jupiter's cupbearer. Her husband had chosen instead the Trojan, Catamitus (Greek Ganymede).

After the destruction of Troy, Aeneas had directed his ships to head west. Somewhere out there was a new home for him and his people.

Slowly, at first, and then with conviction, Juno descended down to Earth and to the island of Aeolus—master of the winds.

"My dear King Aeolus," said Juno.

"My goddess!" Aeolus stood back, amazed at her sudden entrance. "To what do I owe this honor."

Juno looked away for a moment, considering her words carefully, then turned back to him with a look that drilled into his eyes, commanding his full attention, even though she already had it. "I have come to ask a favor. A tiny thing, really. It's trivial, but it needs to be done."

"Yes, my lady?"

"I would like you to use your winds to create a storm. Over there," she pointed out to sea, "are the ships of Aeneas, the Trojan prince, and all his fellow refugees. I want them destroyed—especially the ship holding Aeneas."

"Hmm-mm," Aeolus nodded thoughtfully, then shook his head in disagreement. "My lady, I cannot. I have no grievance with Aeneas or his people."

"But you must," said Juno. "Perhaps I could make the task more attractive by including Deiopea to become your bride."

The king's eyebrows raised in appreciation of the offer. The sea nymph, Deiopea, was said to be the loveliest of all sea creatures. But he shook his head again. "My lady, I will not take her as wife, for I already have one, and she is sufficient for me. But because this means so much to you, I will help."

"Thank you, kind sir," said Juno, and abruptly vanished.

Immediately, Aeolus gathered all his winds and overwhelmed the Trojan fleet. This storm disturbed the surface of the sea, and suddenly, Neptune (Greek Poseidon) was alerted to the commotion in his realm.

"What goes on here?" Neptune demanded. He saw the winds and their target—the Trojan ships. The sea god had no love for Troy, but he resented the intrusion into his domain. "Be still, waters!" he commanded. And he calmed the winds, despite the efforts of Aeolus. This was Neptune's territory, and any intrusion by another god was unwelcome.

Neptune could smell the handiwork of Aeolus and knew someone else was behind this attack. Despite his dislike of the Trojans, he disliked the intrusion even more. So, he gave the ships of Aeneas a favorable breeze which took them to the north coast of Africa, not far from the new town of Carthage.

Aeneas and his fellow travelers landed on the shore, thankful to be alive.

In the distance, Aeneas saw a beautiful woman approaching on horseback. She had a bow strung across her shoulder and a quiver on her back. He watched her as she made her way to them.

"You are all lucky to be alive," said the woman, who happened to be his mother, Venus, in disguise. "Some of the gods favor you and your companions."

"I was beginning to lose hope," said Aeneas. "I appreciate your words, but even I was beginning to wonder if all of the gods might be against us, now that we have lost our war with the Greeks."

"Fear not," she said, "your destiny is to plant the seed of a great empire."

The young prince cocked his head to the side, uncertain he could believe this from some strange huntress on the beach of North Africa.

"And you are in luck," she said. "Not far this way," she pointed toward the West, "there is a new town called Carthage, founded by the Phoenicians of Tyre, and ruled over by good queen Dido. You will usually find her in the Temple of Juno."

"Well, thank you, fair stranger," said Aeneas, just as she prodded her horse into a trot in the same direction. "But—" and she was gone, receding into the distance, ignoring his words.

"I see trees over there, master," said one of his fellow travelers. "There may be a well and clean water."

"Good. Let's us refresh ourselves and then head toward this new town, Carthage."

Aeneas found his way to the Temple of Juno and there entreated the queen to help his small band of refugees. In the tradition of all civilized folk, she invited him and his fellow travelers to a banquet in their honor.

In the meantime, Venus met with her son, Cupid—half-brother to Aeneas.

"My darling son, I need your help. I would like you to help me create a bond between Queen Dido and your brother, Aeneas."

"Yes, mother."

At the banquet which Dido arranged for Aeneas and the other Trojans, Cupid showed up disguised as Ascanius, Aeneas's son by his first wife, Creusa. While the image of the son approached Queen Dido bearing gifts, invisible Venus surrounded the real Ascanius with a ghostly shroud to keep others from noticing there were two of him. Even the real Ascanius was bewitched into ignoring the imposter.

Dido graciously received the gifts and reached for the handsome young boy to draw him close. She felt an overpowering urge to give him a mother's affection. While in Dido's embrace, Cupid worked his charms on her, weakening a sacred pledge she had made to stay faithful to her dead husband, slain by her brother.

"Tell me, Aeneas," said Queen Dido, "all that has happened to you. I want to hear the entire story. Stories help us to understand." She was going to say that stories also entertain, but thought better of it, knowing the Trojan's tale would include great tragedy.

"Well, my lady," said Aeneas, "I would like to thank you for your gracious hospitality. We are weary from our travels. This spot of civilization soothes our souls."

The queen raised her cup toward him and smiled.

"Our once-great city," said Aeneas, "at the entrance to that enormous body of water, northeast of the Mediterranean—what the Greeks call the Euxine Sea—our city was attacked by the Greeks. For ten long years, they tried to destroy us all. Then, on the eve of what seemed like our victory, the Greeks left a gift on our doorstep and departed en masse. But the gift was our undoing, for within it was Greek soldiers who lay as still as death until we were drunk and asleep from our long celebration.

"By the end of the next day, our city was a smoldering mass of former humanity. Our people killed or under Greek subjugation. Some of us escaped inland. The next day, when the hostilities were done, and some semblance of peace returned, I went back to Troy to find my wife, but she was dead. In the smoke, I saw an image of her, and it spoke, telling me I would establish a great city to the West.

"Inspired by her words, I convinced my fellows to help me build our small fleet of ships. Our travels took us all over the Eastern Mediterranean—to Thrace, where we found the remains of our fellow Trojan, Polydorus. Then to Strophades, where we met Celaeno, the Harpy. She told us to leave her island. And before we left, she said I must look for a place called Italy. After that, we landed at Crete. We thought perhaps we arrived at our destination and began to build our city. We named it Pergamea. But then Apollo visited us and told us we had not yet arrived at our true destination.

"At fair Buthrotum, north of Macedonia, we attempted to replicate Troy. On that island, we met the widow of Prince Hector and found Prince Helenus who had also escaped. Now, Helenus has the gift of prophecy. From him, I learned more about my own destiny. He told me I needed to find Italy which is also known as Ausonia, and by the name Hesperia."

"There are two large peninsulas named Hesperia," said the queen. "One is due north of here, across the Tyrrhenian Sea. The other is at the far western end of the Mediterranean, north of the exit to our small, inland sea, and entrance to a far larger, Great Ocean, the realm of Atlas and the once great Atlantis which sank so long ago."

The queen suddenly felt self-conscious about what she had just said. The Phoenician custom was to keep secret the discoveries of the Phoenician people. Such discoveries were frequently made at great cost and to give them away would be to lose the Phoenician hold on such knowledge. But the queen had been feeling exceptionally joyous with the arrival of these guests. She felt overcome with a generous spirit.

"Thank you, my lady, for your help in our quest. After Buthrotum, we found ourselves in a land called Trinacria where our ships barely escaped a grave danger we later learned was called Charybdis—a vast whirlpool which threatened to swallow entire ships. From there, we encountered the Cyclopes and one of the Greeks—a soldier who had served under Ulysses—a soldier who had been left behind in their mad rush to escape the great, one-eyed beasts. We took Achaemenides, the Greek, on board with us, but barely escaped with our own lives when blind Polyphemus heard our voices. Not long afterward, my own father, Anchises, died peacefully of his own years. We sailed next into the open seas, unsure where to find this Hesperia—this Italy. A great storm nearly destroyed us, but then we found the coast not far from here."

"I am so thankful that you made it," said the queen. Her eyes glistened toward him, and at that moment, she knew she loved this prince.

Aeneas, too, could feel the bond and gazed upon her with deep admiration.

Later, after they had taken in their fill. Dido suggested Aeneas, and a few of his best hunters go inland with her to find game.

In the hall, but invisible to these mortals, Juno confronted Venus.

"Listen," said Juno. "I would like to strike a bargain with you. These two seem to be well-suited for one another. See how much they are in love?"

"Yes," said Venus, "what did you have in mind."

"I will stop my attacks on these Trojans if Aeneas stays here in Carthage with Dido, becoming her husband."

Venus smiled at the thought of her son marrying the local queen. This pleased her greatly. And since she already orchestrated the beginnings of love, she would do everything she could to hold Juno to her promise.

During their hunt, Dido and Aeneas followed their clues to find their prey and became separated from the others. And when a storm struck they found a nearby cave for shelter. Within the cave, Aeneas held Dido close to keep her warm. In that embrace, there came kisses and a deeper, more passionate experience which Dido took to mean Aeneas was now bound to her for life.

After they returned to the palace in Carthage, the two were clearly and deeply in love. But their affection was short-lived. While the two were together in her chamber, a bright light appeared in the middle of the room and suddenly there appeared the form of Mercury, messenger of the gods.

"Aeneas, son of Venus," said Mercury, "this has gone too far, and Jupiter himself has commanded me to intervene. You have a destiny, and it must be seen through to the end."

"But," said Dido. "does he have to stay away. Can't he return to me?"

"I'm afraid not, my lady," replied Mercury. "The future fate of the world hangs on the shoulders of Aeneas."

Dido shook her head and screamed in agony. The pain of such fresh love being snuffed out before its full blossom was too much to bear. She looked to Aeneas for some relief from her agony.

"Sorry, my love," was all he could say.

Her screams filled the palace with such remorse all could feel her pain.

Immediately, she grabbed the sword of Aeneas and left the room.

Cautiously, he followed. He could hear her commands to build a pyre in the great opening in front of the palace. When it had been built, she climbed up to the top of it, his sword in her hand.

"People of Carthage. We've all suffered too much tragedy of late. First, the murder of my husband, and now this tragic love that must never be. Suddenly, she plunged the sword into her abdomen.

Her eyes goggled in incredible pain, and she dropped to her knees, the sword sliding from her wound. "There will forever be great strife between our peoples, Aeneas. You have wounded me more than this sword could ever do." She then fell backward onto the pyre, gasping these final words, "rise up from my bones, avenging spirit."

Understanding the gravity of this act, Aeneas quickly gathered his people and ushered them out of the city and back to their ships.

As they sailed away, he looked back at Carthage, but all he could see was the smoke pouring upward into the sky from Dido's funeral pyre.

What History and an Analysis of Myth Tell Us

Estimates for the founding of Carthage range from 1215 to 814 BC. Modern historians seem to favor the later date, because of a reference made by Timaeus of Taormina that Carthage had been founded 38 years before the first Olympiad (776 BC). This is ironic and possibly quite wrong, if we believe the story of Aeneas, because the Trojan

War was supposedly far earlier—traditionally dated at 1184 BC. Some historians placed the founding of Gadir (Roman Gādēs, Moorish Qādis, modern Cádiz, Spain) at about 1104 BC, as a colony of Tyre—far beyond Carthage when traveling from Tyre. While it's entirely possible that Tyre bypassed many locations to establish a lonely outpost beyond the far, opposite end of the Mediterranean, it seems more likely they created at least one or two intermediate colonies across that 4,000-kilometer length. The archaeological level at Hissarlik, Turkey, associated with the Trojan War, called Troy VII was destroyed about 1220 BC.

Though Aeneas has minor mention in Homer's *Iliad* the myth of Aeneas being the grandfather of Rome came about during the first century with writers like Virgil, Ovid, and Livy. So, it seems highly probable the Roman connection to Troy, was contrived to establish a pseudo-historical basis for the Julian family brand.

From this fictionalized narrative, Julius Caesar could claim direct descent from the goddess Venus, through her son, the Trojan Aeneas. In addition, Aeneas's father, Anchises, was fourth grandson of Zeus and Electra. Thus, every time a member of the Caesar family spoke, they were speaking from a position of divine power, and this helped them to command greater respect. It didn't save Julius Caesar from the conspiracy to assassinate him, but it did help to lay the foundation of "gravitas" that grew into the office of emperor.

Venus was the goddess of love, but Julius Caesar had made a name for himself, and his extended family, more from his own acts of war—against the Celtic Gauls, and later against disruptive elements within the Roman Republic.

From these histories (contrived or handed down), we learn which gods favored the Romans and their founders.

Some of the other gods were no friend to Rome and its founding. These defacto enemies of Troy, and thus, by implication, of Rome, were Juno (Greek Hera), Vulcan (Hephaestus), Mercury (Hermes), Neptune (Poseidon), Thetis (no counterpart in Roman mythology), Timorus (Phobos), Formido (Deimos) and Discordia (Eris). Discordia (Eris), after all, was the goddess who had started the entire Trojan problem with her jealous spitefulness for not being invited to a divine wedding. It seems doubly abusive she should be against the party being attacked because of her own behavior. Supporting Troy, and by inference, also Rome, were Venus (Aphrodite), Apollo, Mars (Ares), Diana (Artemis), Latona (Leto) and Greek Scamander (no Roman equivalent).

From the expanded story of Aeneas, by the Romans, we see Jupiter also supported the Roman cause.

From Aeneas, the son of Venus down to the founders of Rome—Romulus and Remus—there were 15 generations of Latins, first at Lavinium and then at Alba Longa.

In the next chapter, we see how these divine, Trojan demigods struggled to establish a beachhead in the middle of the Italian peninsula, amongst numerous other tribes.

Check out this book

BIBLIOGRAPHY

Ancient Sources of Greek Myths:

Apollodorus [Pseudo-Apollodorus]. *The Library.* James George Fraser, trans. London: William Heinemann, Ltd., 1921.

Callimachus. *Hymns and Epigrams, Lycophron and Eratus.* A. W. Mair and G. R. Mair, trans. 2nd ed. Cambridge, Mass: Harvard University Press, 1921.

Hesiod. *Theogony and Works and Days.* M. L. West, trans. Oxford: Oxford University Press, 1988.

Homer. *The Iliad.* Robert Fagels, trans. New York: Viking Penguin, 1990.

——. *The Odyssey.* Robert Fagels, trans. New York: Viking Penguin, 1996.

Moore, Abraham, trans. *The Olympic and Pythian Odes of Pindar.* Boston: Nathan Haskell Dole, 1903.

Nagy, Gregory, trans. "Homeric Hymn to Demeter." <http://www.uh.edu/~cldue/texts/demeter.html> Accessed 12 February 2018.

Oldfather, C. H., trans. *Diodorus of Sicily in Twelve Volumes.* Volume 2: *Books II (continued), 35–IV, 58.* London: William Heinemann, Ltd., 1968.

Pausanias. *Description of Greece.* W. H. S. Jones, trans. Revised ed. Cambridge, MA: Harvard University Press, 1918.

Stewart, Aubrey, and George Long, trans. *Plutarch's Lives.* Vol. 1. London: G. Bell and Sons, 1925.

Modern Writings:

Haar, James. "Music of the Spheres." In *Oxford Music Online: Grove Music Online.* <www.oxfordmusiconline.com> Accessed 16 February 2018.

Wright, Craig. *The Maze and the Warrior: Symbols in Architecture, Theology, and Music.* Cambridge, MA: Harvard University Press, 2001.

Free Bonus from Captivating History
(Available for a Limited time)

Hi History Lovers!

Now you have a chance to join our exclusive history list so you can get your first history ebook for free as well as discounts and a potential to get more history books for free! Simply visit the link below to join.

Captivatinghistory.com/ebook

Also, make sure to follow us on:
Twitter: @Captivhistory
Facebook: Captivating History:@captivatinghistory

Made in the USA
Middletown, DE
19 September 2020